ELEMENTS OF FAITH

ELEMENTS OF FAITH

An Introduction to Orthodox Theology

by
Christos Yannaras

Translated by
Keith Schram

T&T CLARK
EDINBURGH

T&T CLARK
59 GEORGE STREET
EDINBURGH EH2 2LQ
SCOTLAND

First published 1991
Reprinted 1995

ISBN 0 567 29190 1

British Library Cataloguing in Publication Data
Yannaras, Christos
Elements of Faith
1. Catholicism. Doctrines.   2. Orthodox Eastern Church
I. Title
230.042

Typeset by Waverley Typesetters, Galashiels
Printed and bound in Great Britain by Hartnolls Ltd, Bodmin

To Spyridon and Anastasis, a daily legacy

By the same author

The Freedom of Morality, tr. Elizabeth Briere, St Vladimir's Seminary Press, Crestwood, NY 1984 (in English).

Heidegger and Areopagite: On the Absence and Ignorance of God, Ekdoseis <<Domos>> 1987 (in Greek). *De l'absence et de l'inconnaissance de Dieu*, Editions du Cerf, Paris 1971 (in French).

The Metaphysics of the Body. Ekdoseis<<Dodoni>> 1971 (in Greek).

The Modern Greek Identity, Ekdoseis Gregori 1983 (in Greek)

Outline for an Introduction to Philosophy, Ekdoseis<<Domos>> (in Greek).

Philosophie sans rupture, Editions<<Labor et Fides>>, Geneve 1986 (in French).

Person and Eros, Ekdoseis<<Domos>> 1987 (in Greek). *Person und Eros*, Vandenhoeck und Ruprecht-Verlag, Göttingen 1982 (in German).

Proposals for a Critical Ontology, Ekdoseis<<Domos>> 1985 (in Greek).

The Real and the Imaginary in Political Economy, Ekdoseis<<Domos>> 1989 (in Greek).

Truth and the Unity of the Church, Ekdoseis Gregori 1977 (in Greek).

Translator's Introduction

A reader may be surprised by two things about this book: The first is that the references and supporting material he might expect are not present. As Prof. Yannaras indicates in his "Prologue", the audience he wishes to address with this book is not especially the professional theologians for whom such notes would be most desirable. It must be remembered that this book is a summary of many years of reflection and exploration. The footnotes are contained in the previous and often more technical studies that lie behind this work. His views about the epistemological chasm that divides the orthodox and "western" mentalities are set out, for instance, with full documentation in his *Introductory Outline of Philosophy* (in Greek). [1)]

Secondly, we are not accustomed to such strong language in an age of ecumenism. For this reason alone, the book is worth reading. These opinions are not unique to him, although his analysis of the foundational ecclesial differences within Christianity shows a more penetrating and perceptive awareness of the issues than is sometimes encountered in other theologians, whether more polemical or more eirenic. This consciousness leads him to question, in fact, whether our present inter-Church dialogues are not merely dealing with superficial symptoms of a profounder disunity. See especially his book *Truth and the Unity of the Church* (in Greek). Prof.

---

[1] Published in French as *Philosophie sans rupture*, (Genêve, Editions "Labor et Fides", 1986). Two other books by Prof. Yannaras are available: in English, *The Freedom of Morality*, (St Vladimir's Seminary Press, Crestwood, NY, 1984) and in German. *Person und Eros*, Göttingen, Vandenhoeck und Ruprecht Verl., 1982).

Yannaras provides a salutary note of caution to the euphoria of "agreed statements".

It has been my concern to retain the sense of enthusiasm and commitment to the truth of the Church that is so evident in the Greek original of this book. I hope that not too much of his warmth, vigour and directness has been lost. For any errors or infelicities in this translation, I apologize to the reader and to the author.

Keith Schram.

Contents

x

Prologue

This book does not seek to convince anyone of its positions, nor to dissuade any hypothetical opponents. It is not an "apology" for Christian faith, nor does it aim to convert the reader to its views. It has just one ambition: to distinguish what the Christian faith is from what the Christian faith is not. That is, to clear up as much as it can the confusion which seems to exist today in our consciousness relative to the truth of the Christian Church and to purify this truth from the blend of alien and foreign ingredients which tend to substitute themselves for it.

But all this must be done in a way that is simple, comprehensible, and accessible to the "average man", as we put it, and more particularly to the average "intellectual" because it is chiefly he, the intellectual, who is the bearer and the victim of this confusion. Cut off, as a rule, from the experiential roots of faith, perhaps also psychologically oppressed by a ritualistic family religiosity and recollections – usually negative – from a superficial course of catechesis in school, today's intellectual rejects something that he thinks is the faith, while in reality he is ignorant of that faith. But if he wishes at some time to become informed about what it is exactly that he is rejecting, there should still be one small book – a primer or an elementary handbook – written in his own language in which he might find refuge.

This is, however, an audacious undertaking because it is almost impossible to speak about certainties of life with the language of the mind, the language of thought. But to announce the ecclesial faith is, first of all, the same act of love with which the Church "endures all things" (1 Cor 13.7). It is, then, necessary to endure even this "wretched generation of enlightened men", as the poet says.[2] It is, we might say, up to each of us to take aim at the rationalist who is to be found in all of us today. Even love must speak a language which will be comprehensible to today's man caged in his own logic without changing that language into a rationalistic system and which will build a bridge over to his side.

Briefly, this book, which might be more exhaustive or better expressed, offers at least "a primer of faith". The faith expressed in it is the orthodox faith of the Church – no one's private opinions. But the mode of expression and the accent are nevertheless an individual endeavor, with weaknesses and omissions, certainly. To find the right way to present the faith calls for much love. Love is neither emotionalism nor mere good intentions, but rather the supreme struggle for that self-transcendence which is, as the Church puts it, holiness.

If, in spite of all this, someone or other succeeds in reading the faith out of this primer, he will have once again confirmed the paradox of Siloam: with a little mud of the earth, human eyes open to the wonder of life (Jn 9.6-7).

2 T.S. Eliot. *Choruses from "The Rock"*, III, in *Collected Poems 1909-1962*. (London, 1963) p. 181.

1

"Positive" Knowledge and Metaphysics

There are areas of learning or sciences which we call "positive": They claim to be positive, to be assured, to have the character of unquestionable certainty. Anyone can verify them by observation, experiment or mathematical reasoning. They relate to the reality of the world which surrounds us; they are areas of learning or sciences of *physical* reality.

Likewise, the sciences which are occupied with the phenomena of the social life of man and its organization and function, or with reliable information about the past (the *history* of man), present themselves as positive. Here knowledge is immediate, empirically verifiable and, consequently, assured and obligatory for all.

The most basic pursuit of our civilization today seems to be for this assured, positive and unquestionable knowledge. Every detail of our *way* of life, from family upbringing to education in school, to our vocation and the organization of the structures and institutions of our social life presupposes and aims at what we call *objectivity*: firm knowledge, tangible, plain to all.

As an attitude of mind, an atmosphere, or a self-evident necessity, the demand for objectivity marks the man of our time. We grow up learning to value what is *logical*, unquestionably *right*. We are equipped to be objectively right because this is the only standard imposed on us and only this will lead to social recognition and the attainment of concrete goals.

But at the same time, within our rationally organized life there lurk a few questions which it is impossible to submit to the demand for positive knowledge. A first set of such questions is connected with the experiences which we have in the field of art: What is it that differentiates a painting of Rembrandt from a painting of Van Gogh or the music of Bach from the music of Mozart? How does it happen that the artistic creativity of a man persists without being subordinate to any positive predetermination or objective classification? And how do marble, colour, or words "keep the form of man", as the poet says? How do they preserve the uniqueness and dissimilarity of each artist which is impressed on his work?

The very observation of nature gives birth to such questions, which cannot be answered by "positive knowledge", as soon as we go beyond the simple description of objects to wonder about their initial cause and their final purpose: How did all that exists around us come to be and where is it heading? Was it made by someone? Did it come about by chance? Has it always existed and will it continue to exist in the same irrational and inexplicable way? Whatever answer we give will be equally arbitrary and indemonstrable – in any case with the criteria of *positive* knowledge. How is the beauty of the world to be interpreted, the harmony, the order, the organic functionality which serves every tiny detail of the physical world?

Beyond all this, at some moment of our life, some "turn in our road", we will be met inescapably with sickness, decay, death. And then, they pose the most implacable questions: What is the logic of this ephemeral cycle of our biological existence? Does it all just end in two metres of earth? What is it that is extinguished by death and leaves the body a neutral thing to dissolve in the ground? What are a man's look, his reason, his laugh, his gestures, his "expression"? What is extinguished by death is what makes him unique, distinct and unrepeatable – the way he loves, enjoys, hurts, the distinctive way with which each man realizes life. Are these all just biological functions like digestion and breathing and the circulation of the blood, or the conscious and the subconscious and the unconscious, and finally the "ego", the identity of man or whatever else "depth psychology" (as it is called) tries to study today with its scientific attitude? Or maybe man *is*, exists, in a way which is not exhausted with his biological functions and this *way* makes a man truly existent without his being touched by time and death?

At some moment of his life, a bend or "turn in his road", a man suspects that positive knowledge answers only the smallest of his questions and that there exists an area *beyond physics*[1], the metaphysical area (the area of art, of love, of the mystery of existence) which must be approached, if someone is ever to come to know it, using "weights and measures" very different from those which assure the simple description of the perceptible data of nature.

For whole ages man has wrestled and still wrestles with meta-physical questions. Philosophy, art, the religions are forms of this ceaseless and perpetual struggle which distinguishes man from every other existing thing and creates his *civilization*. Today we live in a civilization which tries to lay its foundations by repressing, forgetting, metaphysical questions, though even this posture is once more metaphysical and itself lays the foundations (or lays them again) of a civilization.

Besides, as much as man tries to flee the implacable questions of metaphysics, as much as he undertakes to forget them in the midst of the fever of professional activity, of political service or of the insatiable search for pleasure, as much as he despises them and ridicules them in the name of a mythologized "science" which "has an answer for everything" or "will one day have an answer", still the questions bide their time at some moment on the road. The sudden "breakdown", as Dürrenmatt puts it, an automobile accident, cancer, some cardiac "episode", and the armour of self-sufficiency collapses, the heart-rending nakedness of man is revealed. The chaos of unanswered questions is opened unexpectedly before us and these questions are not just doubts in the mind, but frightening gaps in our existence.

In these unanticipated moments of "metaphysical awakening", one might say that all our questions are summarized automatically in one significant word, spontaneously known and immeasurably unknown: *God*. Who first spoke to us about him? What is he? And where is he? A creature of

---

[1] In Greek, *meta ta physica*. – *tr.*

man's imagination, a necessity which our mind suggests – or a real existence, but hidden like the poet within his words and the artist within his paintings? Finally, does he exist or does he not exist? Is he the cause and goal of existence and of the world? Does man have within himself something from him, something which surpasses space, time, decay, and death?

2

The Problem of God

If we ask ourselves how men began to speak about God, how this problem entered into their life, we shall find three rather basic and very important points of departure:

a. The religious beginning

Religious need is the first point of departure. There is within man, in his own "nature", we might say, a spontaneous need to relate to something which surpasses him, to some existence much superior to his own. Perhaps this need may start from man's fear in face of natural powers which are a threat and a danger to his life. He wants to propitiate these powers, to be reconciled with them and so to restrain the fear which they occasion him. The way for him to do this is to attribute reason to them, to consider them rational existences which can hear him, understand him, accept the gifts which he offers them as sacrifices. Thus, man sees a rational existence, superior, immeasurably great, which hurls thunderbolts and stirs up the seas and shakes the earth and fertilizes seeds and perpetuates life. He calls this power *God* and often sees it as fragmented; he sees as many gods in the world as there are powers which impress themselves on him.

We do not know if this is the most probable motive for the beginning of religion. But certainly we often meet such a level of religiosity in human societies even today. It is an anthropo-centric religiosity: it wishes to assure and to safeguard man in his weakness, to silence his fears. Therefore it is not confined only to a religious *faith* in higher powers, but also offers man specific conduct for his egocentric reassurance and psychological defence. It offers him *worship* with strictly defined forms which assure some contact with and propitiation of the divine, just as it offers him a *morality*, that is, a code of commands and obligations, of what is pleasing to God and what is not.

If a man follows the solemn forms consistently and precisely applies the moral code which his religion imposes, then indeed "he has God in his pocket", that is, he can rest assured that he is managing well in his relationship with the divine. He does not fear punishment; to the contrary, he expects only rewards and services from God. Usually, this form of religious man is very conceited about his piety and virtue and becomes harsh towards all his fellow men who do not display analogous religious and moral achievements.

b. The search for truth

The search for truth and the thirst for knowledge form a second starting point for the human relationship with God.

In all the great civilizations which history knows, the human mind's search for clarification of the foundational philosophical questions has resulted in a *theology*, that is in a "discourse on God". The ancient Greeks provide the most characteristic and most complete example.

In ancient Greece, reference to God is a logical consequence of the observation of the world. When we observe the world, we ascertain that everything that exists follows a logical series and order. Nothing is chance or arbitrary. And so we are obliged to accept that even the origin of the world itself must be a logical result; that is, the world is a result of a concrete cause. This First Cause of Principle of the world we call God.

We are unable to know what this First Cause or Principle of the world is. But we can derive with our reasoning a few conclusions about the properties (characteristics) which it must have: To be a First Cause means that it does not owe its own existence to something prior to itself and, consequently we must assume it to be its own cause, the cause both of itself and of everything that exists.

Since, as Cause of itself it does not depend on anything else, we must consider it to be *absolute* magnitude (absolute: released from, free from every limitation). As absolute magnitude, God should be independent of time, all-powerful, infinite. He must himself be the principle of motion which constitutes the "becoming" of the world and is measured as time. Therefore as the *principle* of motion, he must himself be unmoved in any way, since nothing pre-exists God in order to put him in motion. And as unmoved he is also immutable and, consequently both impassible and perfectly blessed.

None of these conclusions (and many others) which we can derive by thought, make God known to us, they only convince our reason and force us to accept intellectually the assumption of his existence as a reality. It is as if we are walking in the desert and suddenly encounter in front of us a house; we are then obliged to accept the fact that someone has built it – houses do not grow, nor are they erected by themselves in the desert. But we do not know *who* the builder is. From the characteristics of the building we can assume a few properties or distinctive features of the builder, whether he has good taste, for instance, or enough skill in the application of statistics, or even what needs he was serving with the rooms he built. But his face remains unknown to us; we have never met him, we do not know him. Surely he exists but he is inaccessible to our immediate knowledge.

c. The personal relationship

Only one historical tradition preserves the *third* starting point for the human relationship with God, the tradition of the Hebrew people.

The Hebrews begin to speak about God because of a concrete historical event: about nineteen hundred years before Christ, in the land of the Chaldeans (in a region in upper Mesopotamia, near the Persian Gulf) God revealed himself to a specific man, Abraham. Abraham answered God, as we answer a human person, an existence with whom we can converse and before whom we can stand face to face.[1] God

[1] In Greek, the same word, "*prósopo*", serves for "person" and for "face". – tr.

called Abraham to settle in Canaan, because this land was pre-ordained for the people who would issue from his descendants – the children to whom Sarah, already unable to bear children, would give birth.

The knowledge of God which arose from Abraham's personal encounter with him has nothing to do with theoretical assumptions, reductive syllogisms and logical proofs. It was an experience of relationship only and, like every true relationship, it was based only on the faith or trust which is born between those who are in a relationship with one another. God proved his divinity to Abraham only by his faithfulness to his promises. And Abraham trusted God, to the point of being ready to sacrifice the child whom Sarah had given him in her old age – this child who was the presupposition for the fulfillment of the promises of God.

Isaac and Jacob, the son and grandson of Abraham, have the same knowledge of God from immediate experience of a personal relationship with him. So, for the descendants of the family from which the people of Israel arise, God is neither an abstract concept nor an impersonal power. When the Hebrews speak about God, they say, "The God of our fathers". He is "the God of Abraham, of Isaac, and of Jacob", an actual person whom their ancestors knew and with whom they associated. The knowledge of God is based on faith and trust in their ancestors, in the trustworthiness of their testimony.

d. Choice of goal and route

These three starting points for the human relationship with God do not belong exclusively to the past. They exist as real possibilities in every time and in every place. There are always people who accept the existence of God, without being very interested in his truth and the theoretical problems to which it gives birth. They accept it only as a psychological need to relate to something "transcendent", a need for their individual security in face of the unknown, as a need for authority and the observance of an ethical order within the world.

Similarly, there are always people who accept the existence of God, only because their logic obliges them to accept it.

They believe, as they say, "in a higher power", "a supreme Being" which has made everything that exists and sustains them. They cannot know nor, perhaps, does it interest them what this "higher power" or "supreme Being" is exactly. Even if they combine their simple intellectual certainty with a few "religious" customs – with their accommodation to the solemn forms and ethical imperatives of the religion established in the social environment in which they live – within them there remains a deep agnosticism which is incompatible with anything except the general and abstract idea of the "supreme Being" alone.

The third form of relationship with God also exists, faith and trust in the historical experience of his revelation. The "children of Abraham", the people of Israel, continued throughout the centuries their attitude of accepting the truth of God, not with emotional or logical criteria, but only with the certainty of the trustworthiness of their fathers. God proved his existence with his interventions within history, verifying his presence always within the bounds of the personal relationship. He revealed himself to Moses and spoke with him "face to face, as a man speaks to his friend".[2] He called the prophets and enlisted them in the work of reminding the people of the promises to which God always remains faithful.

It is not difficult for those who trust the historical experience of the revelations of God to accept one more intervention of his in the life of men, this time "in the flesh",[3] in the person of Jesus Christ. Certainly for rationalistic thought, the concepts of *divinity* and *incarnation* are contradictory, the one excluding the other. It is not intelligible that God, who by his nature should be infinite, unlimited, all-powerful, etc., should *exist* as a finite, distinct human unit subject to the limitations of space and time. Therefore for the Greeks of the time of Christ, the proclamation of the humanity of God was really "foolishness".[4]

[2]Exodus 33.11 *RSV*
[3]Timothy 3.16 *RSV*; and cf. 1 John 4.2; 2 John 7. – tr.
[4]1 Cor 1.23.

But, for someone to accept or to reject this "foolishness", he must have answered certain fundamental questions, which decide very generally the sense and the content which he gives to life: Is everything that exists predetermined and must it exist in the manner which human logic imposes? Or is existence an event which surpasses the predeterminations and the patterns of the understanding? Can we accept it and study it only with direct experience? What truly exists: what we comprehend with our senses, what our logic confirms? Or do there exist realities which we know within the bounds of a more immediate and general *relationship*? Is this a relationship which permits us, for instance, to distinguish *qualitative* differences, to conceive the "sense" of poetry beyond the words, to bring to awareness the function of symbols, to be assured of our subjective "identity", to reveal the inexpressible uniqueness of a person, to understand the aphorisms of contemporary physics about the "fourth dimension" or about the double interpretation of the nature of light?

These questions are worth more study and detailed analysis, but they will take us far from the basic subject which occupies us. Here we must distinguish principally the ways and paths which we will follow for knowledge of God. If we wish to know the abstract concept of God which logical necessity imposes, we must follow consistently and precisely the rules of logic. If we wish to know the God of the psychology of religion and of the emotions, we must cultivate within ourselves the psychological and religious motives for this knowledge. And if we wish to know the God of the Judeo-Christian tradition, we must follow the way of personal relationship and experience, the way of faith. To follow both one and the other route, to combine the modes of knowledge is the surest route to confusion and impasse.

3

Faith

In most people's consciousness today, the word *faith* has a very specific content: It means the unexamined acceptance of principles and axioms, the assent to theory or teaching which remains unproved. "I believe in something" means that I accept it, even though I do not understand it. I bow my head and submit to an authority which is not always religious, but could also be ideological or political. Religious devotion, ideological discipline and party obedience are often hidden in equal measure under the common mantle of *faith*. There is even a well established watchword of unknown provenance which many think is the quintessence of metaphysics, while it is instead the presupposition of every totalitarianism: "Believe and don't ask questions."

We must say bluntly that such an interpretation of faith has no relation to the meaning which the Judaeo-Christian tradition, at least, gives it. In the framework of this tradition, the word "faith" functions more with the content which it still retains today in business or the market-place than with the concept which the ideologically militant attribute to it.

In fact, when we speak in business about "faith", we still mean today the trust which a merchant inspires in marketing circles. Everyone knows him; they know his conduct and the ethics of his dealings, his record of fulfilling his obligations. If he ever needs to ask for money, he will find a lender immediately, perhaps without collateral for the money which he will get, because his person and his word are a sufficient guarantee.

In the context of the Judaeo-Christian tradition, "faith" functions as it does in business and in the market-place. Here the object of faith is not abstract ideas which derive their validity from some infallible authority. The object of faith is specific persons you are called upon to trust in the context of an immediate experiential relationship.

More concretely: If you believe in God, you do not do so because some theoretical principles suggest this belief to you or some foundational institution guarantees his existence. You believe him because his person, the personal existence of God, gives birth to your trust. His works and his historical "activity", his interventions within history, make you want a relationship with him.

Certainly, the relationship which forms the basis for faith can be direct, but it can also be an indirect relationship, just as with a human person: I believe in someone; I trust him; when I have met him, I know him; I have an immediate relationship with him. But I believe in someone when I do not know him personally, when the evidence of people I trust guarantees his trustworthiness – as I believe in an artist whom I have never known when his own work gives birth within me to trust and admiration for his person.

There are, then, degrees of faith: you proceed from lesser to greater faith, and this progress seems to be an endless journey. However integrated faith may appear, there is always room for growth and maturity. It is a dynamic, always "unperfected perfection". Relative to this, we could say that you begin with trust in the reputation of a person. You proceed to acquaintance with his work and career. An immediate certainty arises when there is a personal meeting, association, direct relationship. It is transformed from simple trust into an absolute surrender of yourself, into an unsparing self-offering, when "eros"[1] and love between us are born. In true eros, the more I

[1] "Ecstatic self-transcendence is, however, referential, an event of relationship and communion. It is *eros* as an ascetical self-denial of individual (existential and intellectual) self-sufficiency, as a general loving self-offering, always revelatory of the uniqueness and dissimilarity of the bounds of personal relationship." C. Yannaras, *Person and Eros*, 4th ed, (Domos, Athens, 1988), p. 10, in Greek. This definition should be held in mind in interpreting the words "eros" and "eros" ("pertaining to erotic") in the text. – tr.

love the more I know the other and I believe in him and surrender myself to his love. Nor does true erotic faith and dedication come to an end, but it is an uninterrupted astonishment at "discoveries" of the other, an always unquenchable study of the uniqueness of his person.

So it is with faith in God. It can begin just with trust in the evidence of people who know him and consort with him and have been permitted the vision of his Face, trust in the testimony of the experience of the partriarchs, saints, prophets, Apostles. It can proceed to the study of the love which his works reveal, the insertion of his revelations within history, his word which leads us by the hand to the truth. Faith is transformed into immediate certainty and surrender of ourselves to his love when we are permitted to know his Face, the uncreated beauty of the light of his glory. Then the "divine eros" which is given birth within us becomes a dynamic transformation of faith "from glory to glory",[2] an uninterrupted astonishment at his revelations, an astonishment which abolishes time.

At whatever level or degree, faith is an event and experience of relationship, a road radically different from intellectual certainty and "objective" knowledge. If we wish to know the God of the biblical tradition, the God of the Church, we must search by the right road, the road of faith. Logical "proofs" for his existence, the objective attempts of apologetics, the historical trustworthiness of the sources of the Christian tradition, can be useful aids in order that the need for faith be born within us. But they do not lead to faith, nor can they replace it.

When the Church calls us to her truth, she does not hold out some theoretical theses which must be accepted in principle. She invites us to a personal relationship, to a *"way"* of life which constitutes a relationship with God or leads progressively and experientially to a relationship with him. This way transforms our entire life from individual survival to an event of communion. The church is a *body* of communion wherein the *members* live, not each one for himself, but each one in an organic unity of love with the rest of the members and with the *head* of the body, Christ. "I believe in the truth of the

[2] 2 Corinthians 3.18.

Church" means that I agree to be included in the "bond of love"[3] which constitutes it; I trust in the love of the saints and of God, and they accept me with faith and trust in my person.

We draw near to God by means of a way of life, not by means of a way of thinking. A way of life includes every function of growth and maturity – it is the way, for instance, which forms the relationship with our mother and father. From nursing and caressing and affection and care to conscious communion and acceptance of their love, there shoots up silently and imperceptibly in the soul of the child faith in his mother and father. This bond does not require logical proofs or theoretical securities, unless this relationship has itself been disturbed. Only then do the arguments of the mind try to substitute for the reality of life.

[3]cf. Colossians 3.14 – tr.

4

Apophatic Knowledge

a. Dogma and heresy

Now, we all know that the Church has her theoretical principles, "dogmas of the faith" as we call them today. Does this not come into opposition with all that we have said above?

Let us look at these things from their historical beginning. Certainly, in the first three centuries of her history, the Church had not produced theoretical formulations of her truth, dogmas which defined her faith. She lived her truth empirically – what her truth *is* was experienced by the members of her body directly and generally, without theoretical refinements. Nevertheless, there was a language – terms, expressions, images – which expressed the ecclesial experience, a language already formed in the first decades of Christian life. It was the language of the Gospels, of the letters of the Apostles, of the texts which the Bishops of the first centuries wrote in order to guide and lead the body of the faithful. But this language had not been driven to theoretical schematization and axiomatic formulations. It merely expressed and marked out that experiential certainty.

What we call today *dogma*, appeared only when heresy came to threaten the experience of the ecclesial truth. The word *heresy* means the choice, selection and preference of one part of the truth to the detriment of the whole truth, the catholic truth. Heresy is the opposite of *catholicity*. The heretics absolutized just one aspect of the experiential certainty of the Church and so inevitably relativized all the others. The procedure of this absolutization was always intellectual – a theoretical preference which usually simplified and schematized the understanding of the ecclesial truth. Classical examples in history . *Nestorianism* and *Monophysitism*. The first absolutized the humanity of Christ, the second his divinity. And in both cases, they relativized and finally destroyed the one entire truth of the incarnation of God, of the God-manhood of Christ. Nestorianism preached an ethical model of a perfect man, Monophysitism an abstract idea of a fleshless God.

The Church reacted to heresies by marking out the terms of her truth, by defining, that is, her experiential expertise. It is very characteristic that the first designation that was given to what today we call dogma was a *definition*, that is, a limit, a boundary of truth. Today's "dogmas" were the definitions of the Ecumenical Councils – those theoretical decisions which formulated the truth of the Church, fixing a *border* between this truth and its corruption by heresy.

b. The limits of experience

Perhaps an example accessible to experience could elucidate the function of definition or limits of truth. Let us suppose that someone appears who claims that *maternal love* means relentless strictness and wild daily beating of a child. All of us who have a different experience of maternal love will protest about this distortion and will oppose to it a *definition* of our own experience: For us maternal love is affection, tenderness, care, all combined with a judicious and constructive strictness.

Up to the moment when this falsification of the truth of maternal love appeared, there had existed no need to *define* our experience. Maternal love was something self-evident to us all, an experiential knowledge objectively indeterminate but also commonly understood. The need for a limit or definition is connected with the threat that maternal love may begin to be considered something other than what we all believe it to be.

But the definition simply signifies or marks off the limits of our experience, it cannot replace it. A man who has never in his life known maternal love (because he is an orphan or for some other reason), can know the definition but cannot know maternal love itself. In other words, knowledge of formulas and definitions of truth is not to be identified with the knowledge of truth itself. Therefore even an atheist can have learned to know well that the God of the Church is triadic, that Christ is perfect God and perfect man, but this does not mean that he knows these truths.

c. Apophaticism

Thus we attain the understanding of the attitude or way in which the Church faces the knowledge of her truth – a stance and way which, in accord with established usage, we call the *apophaticism* of knowledge. Apophaticism means our refusal to exhaust knowledge of the truth in its formulation. The formulation is necessary and required, because it *defines* the truth, it separates and distinguishes it from every distortion and falsification of it. Therefore for the members of the Church the limits or dogmas are the given "fixed points" of truth, which do not admit of changes or differentiated versions in formulating them. At the same time though, this formulation neither replaces nor exhausts the knowledge of the truth, which remains experiential and practical, a way of life and not a theoretical construction.

The apophatic attitude leads Christian theology to use the language of poetry and images for the interpretation of dogmas much more than the language of conventional logic and schematic concepts. The conventional logic of everyday understanding can very easily give man a false sense of a sure knowledge which, being won by the intellect, is already exhausted by it, completely possessed by it. While poetry, with the symbolisms and images which it uses, always exhibits a sense from within the words and beyond the words, a concept which corresponds more to common experiences of life and less to cerebral conceptions.

d. Figurative language

In the texts of the theologians and Fathers of the Church concepts often contradict one another conceptually in order that the transcendence of every representation of their content may become possible, and that the possibility of empirical participation of the whole man (and not only the mind) in the truth expressed therein may show through the logical antitheses. The God of the Church is "Being beyond all being, Divinity more than divine, the nameless name, beginning beyond all beginning, mind beyond the power of thought and word unspoken and the uncontained which contains all things". The knowledge of God is "knowledge in ignorance, participation in what cannot be shared". Theology is the "form of the formless, shaping of shapeless things, symbols of the non-symbolic, forms of things without form"; it expresses "dissimilar similarities drawing everything into its eternal embrace". Truth is identified with immediate experience, Theology with the "vision of God", this "unperfected perfection". The theologians who see God "see the inexpressable beauty of God himself invisibly. They hold without touching; without understanding, they understand his imageless image, his formless form, his shapeless shape, in a visionless vision and an uncompounded beauty, at the same time simple and varied."[1]

It is not accidental that the undivided Church of the first eight centuries and its historical continuity in Orthodoxy in the East based its *catechesis* of the faithful, that is the announcement and transmission of her truth, chiefly on the liturgy. From the liturgical cycle of the Church's services (vespers, matins, the Liturgy, the hours) theology became a poem and a song – experienced more than thought out by syllogistic inferences. Initiation into the truth of the Church is participation in her way of life, in a festive gathering of the faithful, in the visible actualization and revelation of the new humanity which has conquered death.

e. Greek philosophy and Christian experience

Perhaps it is superfluous to add this, but to avoid any possible wrong interpretation, we must say it: The priority of empirical

[1]The last phrases are from Symeon the New Theologian (*Book on Ethics*, Sermon 4 § 37, Sources chrétiennes, 129, pp. 68–70).

participation in relation to the intellectual approach to ecclesial truth means neither a cloudy mysticism and refuge in emotional exaltations, nor to overlook and devalue logical thought. We must not forget that the first Church was born and developed within the boundaries of the Greek world, of the hellenized Roman Empire. And the mentality and psychological makeup of the Greeks was incompatible with obscure mysticism and naïf sentimentality. On the contrary, the Greek sought from the new experience of ecclesial life answers to his own problems and questions – questions which the ancient Greek and hellenistic philosophical tradition had formulated and investigated in a remarkable manner, unique in the history of man.

The Greek mind demanded that it express the Church's truth with its own speech. This demand constituted a very sharp historical challenge as much for hellenism as for the Church. It was a dramatic meeting of two attitudes to life essentially opposed to one another, which gave birth to the great heresies of the first centuries. But the solutions which were provoked because of these heresies, determined the possibilities for survival of Greek philosophy within the limits of life of the Christian world. The two parties which met (Greek philosophy and Christian experience) represented an astonishing dynamic of life, which finally transformed the antithesis into creative synthesis; the Christian Church succeeded in answering with her own given experience the philosophical questions of the Greeks. And Greek philosophy demonstrated the possibilities of its own language and method in the verification of the new understanding of existence, the world and history. The result was an excellent achievement of Greek reason which, without betraying Christian truth and the *apophatic* knowledge of this truth, remained absolutely consistent with the demands for philosophical formulations, thus actualizing a radical break in the whole history of philosophy. The Greek Fathers of the Church in uninterrupted succession from the second to the fifteenth centuries were the pioneers of this achievement.

5

God as Trinity

a. The Biblical testimony

The God of the Church is the God of historical experience, not the God of theoretical assumptions and abstract syllogisms. Precisely this experience of the Church confirms that the God who is revealed in history is not a solitary existence, an autonomous monad or individual essence. He is a Trinity of hypostases, three Persons with absolute existential difference, but as well a community of essence, will and activity.

In the tradition of Israel recorded in the books of the Old Testament, we have clear models and foreshadowing of the truth of the Triadic God. In the narrative of the creation of the world, while everything is constituted by the word of God alone, by his creative command, the decision to create man is unexpectedly expressed in the plural number. It is an expression of the common will of more than one person: "Let us make man in our image and likeness" (Gen 1.26). And when Abraham meets God near the oak of Mamre, he has in front of him three men whom he addresses, however, as if they were one: "God appeared to him at the oak of Mamre, while he was sitting at the door of his tent at noon. Lifting up his eyes he looked and there were three men standing over him and, when he saw them, he ran from the door of his tent to meet them and he fell down on the ground worshipping and said, 'Lord, if ever I have found favour before you ...' " (Gen 18.1-3).

These pictures and models become direct historical revelation in the period of the New Testament. The disciples hear

Christ talking about God his Father and about the Spirit of God, the Paraclete. Three of them – Peter, James and John – are permitted to hear the voice of God the Father on Mount Tabor and to be included within the luminous darkness of the Spirit's presence (Mk 9.2-8). The same thing happens when John the Forerunner and his disciples, at the moment when Christ is baptized in the Jordan, hear the voice of the Father who confirms the sonship of Jesus and see the Spirit descending on the one being baptized, somewhat like a white fluttering of a bird, like a dove (Mk 1.9-11). These are experiences of a presence with perceptible immediacy, but without limitation on the form of the individual object. Therefore they can be stated only in images: a voice like thunder from the sky (Jn 12.27), and a descent of the Spirit like the heavens opening, being rent (Mt 3.16; Mk 1.10), or like a luminous cloud which hides the disciples (Mt 17.5; Mk 9.7; Lk 9.34), or like a violent gust of wind and tongues of fire which rest on them (Acts 2.2-3).

The record of the experiences and the preaching of the first apostolic community preserve the teaching of Christ about the truth of the Triadic Divinity in a similar way. Christ clearly distinguishes himself as Son from his Father: he came to earth "in the name of the Father" (Jn 5.43) and in order to realize the will of the Father and the commandments of the Father (Jn 4.24; 5.30; 15.10), to disclose his Name to men and to do His work (Jn 17.5-6). He converses with his Father in prayer (Mt 11.25; 26.39; Jn 17.1-25) and surrenders his spirit to him when he dies on the cross (Lk 23.46).

At the same time, however, he affirms that "I and the Father are one" (Jn 10.31) and "all that the Father has is mine" (Jn 16.15), without this unity abolishing their separate existential identity, since Christ asks his Father on behalf of the disciples "that all may be one. Just as you, Father, are in me and I in you, so may they be one in us … as we are one" (Jn 7.21-23).

With the same clarity Christ distinguishes the existence of the Paraclete, who is the holy Spirit and Spirit of truth, both from the Father and from himself. He announces his coming in advance and asserts that "he will testify concerning me" (Jn 15.26), "he will teach you all things" (Jn 14.26), "he will lead you into all truth" (Jn 14.26). But as the Son "can do nothing by himself" (Jn 5.19), so the Paraclete "will take from what is mine and declare it to you" (Jn 16.14). The expressions chosen plainly exhibit three different Existences, three Persons of Divinity, without it appearing that the Existences constitute autonomous individuals, and these expressions are quite typical of the gospel text. The Persons of the Trinity do not exist each for himself, they do not claim existential autonomy. On the contrary, the unity of life, will and activity of the Triadic God, of the three divine Persons, is made plain in the words of Christ.

Thus, Christ affirms that for himself God is Father, begetter, and consequently Source and Cause of his existence as Son and Word of God. But the Father is also the Source and Cause of the existence of the Paraclete. If the Son is the Word of God, the Paraclete is the Spirit of God, "who proceeds from the Father" (Jn 15.26); he has his procession, his existential origin and derivation from the Father. But the sending of the Paraclete into the world expresses the common will and activity of the Triadic Divinity. The expressions of the gospel text are again typical: "the Paraclete, whom I will send to you from the Father" (Jn 15.26), "I will ask the Father and he will give you another comforter, the Spirit of truth" (Jn 14.16-17), "the Holy Spirit whom the Father will send in my name" (Jn 14.26). Similar biblical expressions of the common will and activity of the Trinity also apply to the incarnation of the Word, Christ's becoming man: God the Father sends his Son into the world and the Holy Spirit accomplishes the incarnation "overshadowing" the Virgin Mary.

b. The philosophical challenge

None of these expressions and formulations of the Scripture pertaining to the Triadic God of the Church are related to philosophical problems; they are not intended to answer theoretical questions nor to draw their terms and concepts from the language of philosophy. They are an unaffected record of the historical experience of the first apostolic community and the tradition of the words of Christ which illuminate this experience.

But the temptation of philosophical requirements lay in wait in every area of life in the hellenic world within which the Church was born and spread out. This experience was an insuperable scandal wherever the trained mind of the Greeks ran into it. God, in order to be God, must be an absolute and limitless Being. How, then, can it happen that there exist *three* absolute Beings? Each one, in order to be absolute, must infringe the absolute character of the other; the absolute and multiplicity are two contradictory concepts.

The most ingenious and most accommodating answer to the question was first formulated by Sabellius, a hellenized Roman intellectual at the beginning of the third century. For Sabellius, the God of hellenistic philosophy, the absolute and unlimited Being, is the same as the God of the Church. The three Persons which the historical experience of the Church affirmed are just three masks, three different modes of appearance and activity of the one God: specifically, God appears and acts in the Old Testament as Father, in the New Testament as Son, in the life of the Church as Holy Spirit.

Of course, this answer of Sabellius is not an original invention of his. Sabellius just summarizes and systematizes theological speculation which was known at that time in the West by the name of *monarchianism*. Monarchianism (from the word "monarchy", a monad, having a single principle) tried to reconcile the triplicity of the Christian God with the logical requirement of a single transcendent *Principle* to constitute the "essential Divinity". The Roman mind never ceased to be characterized by the attempt at such an accommodation. It always had a propensity for rationalism and schematization and for this reason it labored so productively in legal science.

Further, Sabellius did nothing more than employ the term *person* for the Holy Trinity with the meaning which it had at that time both in the Greek and Latin languages: The Greek word "prosopon" (like its Latin translation "persona") meant precisely the mask which actors wore at the theatre.

The Christian Churches bluntly rejected the interpretation of Sabellius, and the reaction was especially strong in the East.

The experience of the Church and the testimony of the Holy Scripture confirmed the real differentiation of three Existences and the separate existential indentity of each one, of Existences who converse among themselves, the one referring to the other while clearly distinguishing itself, its "hypostasis", that is, as a real entity. The theory of "masks" contradicted both the plain sense of the words of Christ in the Gospels and the experiential relation of the Church to the Person of the Father and to the Person of the Son and to the Person of the Paraclete.

However, Sabellianism (the teaching of Sabellius), even if it was rejected by the Church, continued to spread as a theory and to win partisans. It had the advantage of easily satisfying human logic, because it offered a simplified schematic interpretation of how the God of the Church is both One and Three.

At the end of the third century, Sabellianism had spread into Libya and the strife which it created there provoked the intervention of the theologians and clergy of neighbouring Alexandria. Now at last everyone was using the terms of Greek philosophy. The Alexandrians spoke about the one *Essence* of God and the three *Hypostases*: of the Father, of the Son and of the Spirit, while western theologians insisted on the one *Hypostasis* of God and the three *Persons* of his historical revelation. In this formulation of the West the Alexandrians saw the survival of the heresy of Sabellius, while western writers feared in the formulation of the Alexandrians the danger of Tritheism.

Within these debates at the beginning of the fourth century was born *Arianism*, the heresy which shook the whole Roman empire for decades. Arius was a priest in Alexandria and an enthusiastic opponent of the ideas of Sabellius. Wishing to defend the real existence of the three Persons of the Holy Trinity, but at the same time to remain consistent with the demands of philosophical thought, he began to teach that it is necessary to distinguish not simply different Hypostases, but also different Essences in the case of the Persons of the divine revelation.

He said, then, that the Son is not *consubstantial* (of the same Essence) with the Father, but of a different *created* essence, that God created him before every other creature. So, while he fought Sabellianism he fell himself into the same trap of the requirements of rationalistic thought, accepting a single divine Essence and degrading the Son to a "creature", something produced.

We will not insist further on the historical data. What we have offered up to here was necessary to show only what historical need led the Church to interpret the experience of the Triadic God with the language of philosophy. In fact, the Greek Fathers of the Church finally corrected this interpretation, neither infringing the empirical certainty of the Church in the least, nor refusing the aid of Greek philosophy, mainly in language or terminology and in method.

In any case, the three great Cappadocian Fathers – Basil of Caesarea, Gregory Nazianzen and Gregory of Nyssa – are pre-eminent in this work of correction. But we should note as forerunners and founders of the work of the Cappadocians Ignatius of Antioch, Irenaeus of Lyons and Athanasius of Alexandria. As a successor and the creator of the fullest philosophical synthesis, we note Maximus the Confessor whose own work was anticipated by Leontius of Byzantium and Theodore Raithenus. It was brought to a systematic completion by John Damascene and Photius the Great to culminate in the last great flowering of Greek theology in the 14th century with Gregory Palamas and Nilus and Nicholas Cabasilas.

c. The linguistic "flesh" of truth

The Ecumenical Councils adopted the teaching of the Greek Fathers and established it as the definition or limit of the truth of the Church. The conscience of the faithful recognized in their persons a work analogous to that of the Holy Mother of God: Just as she offered her body for the historical incarnation of the Son and Word of God, so the Fathers offered their astonishing intellectual gifts, with holiness and purity of judgement, in order that the truth of the revelation of God take on the historical "flesh" of the language of men.

But here a further digression is necessary: Why did the Fathers take up the language of Greek philosophy? Did they not make the formulation of the truth of the Gospels more difficult? Did they not make it more difficult for simple people to approach?

These questions arise today when philosophy and the language of philosophy are objects which occupy relatively few people with special learning and academic interests, as we usually say. But the situation was not the same at the time of the Fathers. One could state that in the Greek world, from classical antiquity to the Byzantine period, philosophical problems interested a very wide range of people and provoked discussion among people of all levels of sophistication and from all social classes. The whole culture of the Greeks, both in the pre-Christian and also the Christian periods, was founded on the absolute priority of *truth* and on the investigation of truth. Today we live in a culture which gives priority to *utility* and not to truth. Hence, it is politics and not philosophy which attracts the attention of all social classes, and so we find it more difficult to understand how it was possible at the time of the Fathers for simple people to discuss in the streets and stores the *consubstantial* and *three-personed* God or the difference between essence and hypostasis. But a Byzantine would perhaps have the same astonishment if he heard an "orthodox" Marxist worker today discussing with his Trostkiïte or Maoist colleague the concepts of "surplus capacity" or the accumulation of capital".

We will now try to set out here the teaching of the Christian Tradition (the teaching of the Fathers and the decisions of the Councils) concerning the Triadic God, with a language that is simple and accessible to today's man.

d. Essence and hypostasis

The God of ecclesiastical experience is *One* and *Triadic*. For understanding the truth of the One God, the Church appropriates for its use the philosophical concept of one *Essence* (*Ousía*).

For the definition of the three-fold state of God, it uses the concept of three *Hypostases* or *Persons*. So for the Church, God is *consubstantial* (one Essence – *homoóusios* and *tri-hypostatic* (three Hypostases or Persons).

We have appropriated the concept of essence for our use because this word means the fact of *participating* in *being*. In Greek, the word for "essence" (*ousía*) is derived from the feminine participle of the verb "to be". But in the case of God we cannot speak about participation in being, but about Being itself, the fullness of every possibility for existence and life. Therefore the apophatic formulation "Being beyond all being" which the Fathers often use is closer to the expression of the truth of the God of the Church.

Nevertheless, the distinction between Essence and Hypostases of Essence makes it easier for the Church to "define" and describe the experience of the revelation of God. We may somehow understand more clearly what it is that this distinction means to define if we think that man, formed "in the image" of God, is also one Essence (consubstantial) and a multitude of hypostases or persons (multi-hypostatic). We derive the concept of one essence from the whole set of properties and marks which characterize each man: Each man has reason, thought, will, judgement, imagination, memory, etc. All of us share these common ways in existence, in being; we have a common essence. But every particular realization (hypostasis) of this Being, that is, each man separately, incarnates all the common marks of our essence in a unique, different and unrepeatable way: He speaks, thinks, decides, imagines in a manner absolutely *other* (different to any other man). Each human existence has absolute *otherness*.

We speak, then, of an essence, which however, whether in the case of God or in the case of man, does not exist apart from the specific person who gives it subsistence. Persons hypostasize essence, they give it an hypostasis, that is, real and specific existence. Essence exists only "in persons"; persons are the *mode of existence* of essence.

Again, this does not mean that essence is simply an abstract concept (the concept of Divinity or of humanity) which is formed only in the mind of man as a summary of common properties and marks. We say that essence does not exist except incarnate in concrete persons, but, especially in the case of man, the specific persons (all of us) have a real experience of differentiation of our personal hypostasis from our essence or nature:[1] We often sense that there exist in us two desires, two wills, two needs which seek to be satisfied. The one desire, will or need expresses our *personal* choice and preference, while the other is a *natural* urge (tendency or propensity) which fights against the first and appears as an *impersonal* (instinctive, as we say) demand which leaves no room for free thought, judgement and decision. The Apostle Paul notes this division when he writes to the Romans: "I see in my members another law at war with the law of my mind .... For I do not do what I want, but I do the very thing I hate .... I can will what is right, but I cannot do it" (Rom 7.15-23, *RSV*).

In the following pages of this book, we will speak more analytically about the "rebellion" of human nature against the freedom of the person, the impulse of our nature to exist, to maintain itself and to survive by itself, only as nature, not as personal otherness and freedom. And we will see that this division of nature and person constitutes the failure ("sin") of man's existence,. with death as its final consequence. For the present here we are interested in the truth of nature or essence, which we will study in the case of man as an existential experience of antithesis in the freedom of the person. In the case of God, though, we have nothing given for the study of his Essence; we believe only that no antithesis of nature and person exists there, since failure and death do not exist there. We dare to say (always relatively, within the finite capacity of human language) that the existential fullness of the divine nature harmonizes perfectly with the freedom of the divine Persons, and therefore there is a common divine will and activity and unbreakable unity of life in the Trinity. Unity both of nature and of freedom, a freedom which unites the nature to the life of love. Love constitutes the *being* (*eînai*) of Divinity. But we cannot know what the Essence of Divinity is

---

[1] The two terms "essence" and "nature" are usually used with the same conceptual content.

exactly which the three Persons hypostasize. It transcends not only the abilities of our language, but even our capacity to comprehend the limits of our experience. We are speaking, then, of the incomprehensible mystery of Divinity, the unfathomable truth of the divine Essence.

e. The person

We do not know what God is in his Essence, but we do know the mode of his existence. God is a personal existence, three specific personal existences of whose personal difference the Church has direct historical experience.

We must stop here again: What exactly is a personal existence? What does "person" mean? It seems difficult to define and the definition is, perhaps, finally unattainable. Even in the case of man, where bodily individuality makes "person-hood", the personal elements of human existence, concrete and immediately accessible, it hardly seems feasible for us to define objectively what it is which constitutes personhood, which imparts a personal character to existence.

In principle certainly, there is an answer which it is usual to give to these questions: We all understand that what differentiates personal existence from every other form of existence is *self-consciousness* and *otherness*. We call the awareness of our own existence "self-consciousness", the certainty that I have that I exist, and that it is I who exist, a being with identity, an identity which differentiates me from every other being. And this differentiation is an absolute otherness, a unique, distinct, and unrepeatable character which defines my existence.

Nevertheless, the awareness of one's existence, the ego, the identity, the consciousness of absolute otherness in not plainly and simply a product of the mind, a result of a function of the brain which we call understanding. Self-consciousness is something much more than an intellectual certainty; it has "substrata" which are explored by a whole science, depth psychology, and which are called subconscious, unconscious, ego, superego. In countless ways it tries to define this ultimately intangible and indeterminate something which *is* man, beyond bodily functions and bio-chemical reactions and irritation of cells or any other objective interpretations.

By means of analyses of dreams, of associations, of automatic behavior, and by reference to childhood experiences, to the first relations with the family environment, depth psychology tries to trace the way in which the ego is formed and matures, and this way that the ego both is formed and matures is nothing other than relationship, reference. It is the potential which *constitutes* man, the potential to be *opposite* someone or something, to have one's *face-toward* someone or something, to be a *person*.[2] It is the potential to say "I", addressed to "you", to converse, to share. The person is not an arithmetic unit, an atom from a whole, an entity in itself. He exists only as a self-conscious otherness, consequently only *in comparison with* every other existence, only in relation to, in connection with.

Therefore only the direct relationship, encounter, reference can make a person known. No objective information is able to exhaust the dissimilarity of the person, to make the person known to us. Whatever detailed descriptions we give, as long as we insist on the quantitative nuances of individual traits and properties (physiological characteristics, temperament, character, etc.), what we determine will, in any case, be the same for many individuals, because it is impossible with objective formulations of our everyday language to mark off the uniqueness and dissimilarity of a person. Therefore we must separately evaluate the importance of the function of the *name*, which alone can signify this uniqueness, which alone can express and reveal a person beyond all concepts and determinations.

f. The experience of relationship

If by means of all these descriptions and analyses, we have somehow sketched out and described the experience of

---

[2]The prefix *"prós"* ("to", "toward") together with the noun *"óps, ópos"*, which means "look", "eye", or "face", forms the compound word *"prósopon"*, "face", or "person".

approaching the truth of the person, then we can say that the Church has this experience in her encounter and relationship with the Hypostases of Divinity. We have seen that from the beginning the experience of the patriarchs of Israel confirmed the personal character of Divinity: They meet him "person to person", they speak with him "face to face". The God of Israel is the true God, that is, the really existing, living God, since he is the God of *relationship*, of personal immediacy. Whatever is beyond the possibility of a relationship, what is unrelated, is also non-existent, even if human logic confirms its existence. On Mt Horeb, Moses asks God himself to reveal his personal identity to his people by declaring his Name (Ex 3.13-14). "I am the One who is", answers God, and Moses announces to the people that Yahweh (the "I am") sends him and calls the Israelites to worship "He who is". The divine Name is not a noun which would classify God among beings, nor an adjective which would attribute a characteristic feature. It is a verb, it is the echo on the lips of people of the Word by which God defines himself as existent, as the only pre-eminent existent.

God defines himself as existent from within the limits of a relationship with his people; the revelation of his Name as existent is a covenant relationship with Israel. For the Israelites God is not obliged by his Essence to exist; his existence is not a logical necessity. He is existent because he is faithful to his covenant relationship with his people; his existence is confirmed by faithfulness to a relationship, that is, by the personal immediacy of his revelation and his interventions in the history of Israel.

g. The revelation of life

In the New Testament, this revelation is consummated: God is the really existing One, since he is the *Father*, since he is a personal God – personal not only "in relation to" man, but in relation to his own Being, "in relation to" his Son and his Spirit. Whatever relates to God springs from this relationship of fatherhood, of sonship and of procession, from the truth of the *Persons* which this relationship presupposes, not from

logical conclusions from the concept of God, not from the
necessary and obligatory properties of the Essence of God.

When Jesus manifests himself as the Son of God, he reveals
that "Father" is the name which expresses in the most
profound way the hypostasis of God, what God really *is*: He is
one who begets, a life-giving principle, the possibility for a
relationship to begin which *hypostasizes* being (gives being an
hypostasis). In the Gospels, Christ reveals that the fatherhood
of God has in principle a *unique* character: it corresponds to the
only Son, who is the "beloved" (Mt 3.17), the one in whom the
Father "is well pleased" (Lk 3.22), he whom "he loved before
the foundation of the world" (Jn 17.24). And love is the
assurance par excellence of freedom, the revelation par
excellence of *personal* existence, free from every predetermination of essence or nature.

God the Father "begets" God the only Son, which means:
the Person of the Father *hypostasizes* his own Essence
(Divinity) in a loving relationship with the Son. The unity of
the divine Being (the One God) does not constitute a logical
necessity, but a unity of freedom and love. It is a unity of wills
(Jn 5.30) and of activities (Jn 5.17-20) of the Father and the
Son, their co-inherence (Jn 10.38; 14.10; 17.21), a reciprocal
intimate relationship of knowledge and of love (Jn 12.28;
13.31; 17.4).

Nevertheless, the unique character of the fatherhood of
God is not exhausted in the diadic relationship with the only
Son; this relationship is not a polarization of life with two co-
inhering parts. The unity of the Father with the Son is
universally life-giving; it is the "real life" and the fullness of
life, because the Father is also the one from whom the Holy
Spirit proceeds. In a hypothetical schema of our human logic,
we could say that without the generation of the Son, God
would be a transcendent Monad. And without the procession
of the Spirit, he would be a person "hidden" in a strictly
private relationship, a relationship unrelated to whatever is not
God, but a relationship as well which merely defines the cause
without constituting the *mode* of life.

We say this, not in order to impose our own logical schema
on the truth of God, but in order to express the historical

experience of revelation: The Holy Spirit effects in history the revelation of the Word of God, the incarnation of the Person of the Word, and the formation of the Body of the Person of the Word (which is the Church). All these are always events *giving life* to what is created, events with final reference to the Person of the Father, the image and manifestation of whom is the Son and Word. In his revelation through the Word within creation, within history, and from within the texts of the Scripture, God is confirmed as Father of every personal existence which will accept *adoption*, will agree to realize the same relationship of life with God which the Son has with the Father. But the relationship of adoption is a work of the Spirit, his own procession from the Father establishes sonship as a lifegiving relationship for every existent. He is the "spirit of adoption, in whom we cry 'Abba, Father'. This spirit bears witness with our spirit that we are children of God … coheirs with Christ" (Rom 8.15-17).

h. The lifegiving principle

The Church, passing from the level of activity to the level of existence, understands the texts of the Holy Scripture as testimony and revelation of the *mode* with which he not only acts, but also *is* God. We have said somewhere above that the Cappadocian Fathers in their theology first realized a radical break in the whole history of philosophy. But this new Greek philosophical synthesis which the Fathers achieved is above all a commentary on the biblical texts, with absolute faithfulness both to the spirit and to the letter of the texts.

Where does the radical break lie about which we are speaking? In one phrase we would say: in the identification of hypostasis with person. Person for the Fathers is the hypostasis of being; personal existence makes being a reality. For the first time in human history, being, existence in general, is considered neither something self-evidently given, nor something subject to a predetermined ground or mode of actualization (a substance). What subsists is not predetermined in its hypostasis by its given essence.

A simple example will show us how ancient Greek thought functioned on this subject, and how philosophy continues to function, in many cases, in the West.

When I want to construct a paper-knife, first I must conceive in my mind the concept of a paper-knife, the whole of the characteristics (purposes) which characterize a paper-knife, that is, its given essence. The essence, "paper-knife", precedes and the construction of an actual paper-knife follows. The construction hypostasizes (makes a substance of or gives a concrete existence to) the given essence of the paper-knife.

If we investigate the example, we will have to agree that every existent is the hypostasis (realization) of a general essence. This precedes and defines the mode and purpose of the particularity of every existent. God, then, if he is really existent, is himself an hypostasis of a given essence, his existence realizes (hypostasizes) the given mode and principle of his essence.

In other words, what exists *before* the concrete existence (the possibility of existence, the possibility of being) is a *logical* necessity, certain given principles or modes or essences or ideas to which the realization (hypostasis) of each concrete existence is subject, even that of God himself. Plato spoke very definitely about a "world of ideas, or essences" which contain the logical "models" of every existence and pre-exist that of God himself.

The Church, in the teaching of her Fathers, radically rejects this theory. It is not the *essence* which precedes and defines the existence, but it is the *person* who constitutes the initial possibility of existence, the beginning possibility of being. The person precedes, as self-consciousness with absolute otherness, that is, with absolute freedom from every necessity, from every predetermination of cause, mode or essence.

For the Church, the personal God is the initial possibility of existence, the source and cause of being. God is not in principle a given Essence, which exists in consequence as a Person. Rather he is in principle a Person, who being absolutely free from every necessity and every predetermination hypostasizes (makes into hypostases) his *Being*, his Essence, giving birth eternally to the Son and sending forth the Holy Spirit. The

Person of God the Father precedes and defines his Essence; he is not predetermined by it. God is not obliged by his Essence to be God; he is not subject to the necessity of his existence. God exists, since he is the Father, the one who affirms freely his will to exist, giving birth to the Son and sending forth the Spirit. He exists, since he loves and love is only an event of freedom. Freely and from love, the Father ("timelessly and lovingly") hypostasizes his Being in a Triad of Persons, constitutes the principle and mode of his Existence as a community of personal freedom and love.

i. Freedom and love

The consequences of this truth are important. The principle, source, or starting point of existence is not an impersonal logical necessity; it is not the abstract pre-existence of a divine Essence; it is not the blind urge of an impersonal, absolute Nature. It is the freedom of a Person who actualizes existence, since he loves. Thereafter, the properties which we attribute to God within the range of possibilities of our own logic and language do not have to be considered traits which are imposed on the divine Existence by his Essence or Nature, but consequences of the mode of personal existence.

And so, God is *uncreated*, not because his Essence ought to be uncreated, but because he is "really a Person", an Ego of existential self-consciousness free from any predetermination, and consequently from every provenance, createdness or consequence. He is *timeless*, eternal and without beginning or end, precisely because his personal Existence constitutes the *beginning* and the *end* (purpose) of his Being. He does not tend to become what his essence pre-arranges, so that the tendency and direction of his existence toward his essential end (purpose) might constitute a temporal duration. He is *infinite* and *unlimited*, "transcending place", because the personal mode of his existence is the continuous community of love; he exists as love, not as an autonomous individuality, and therefore he does not stand apart, creating a distance and consequently measurable dimensions. The existence of the Person of God is an uninterrupted closeness, without boundary, limit, or dimension.

Holy Scripture assures us that "God is love" (1 Jn 4.16). It does not tell us that God *has* love, that love is an attribute, a property of God. It assures us that what God *is* is love, that God *is* as love, that the mode by which God *is* is love. God is a Trinity of Persons and this Trinity is a Monad of life, because the life of the hypostases of God is not a simple survival, a pathetic event of maintaining existence, but a dynamic actualization of love, an unbroken union of love. Each Person exists not for himself, but he exists offering himself in a community of love with the other Persons. The life of the Persons is a "co-inherence" of life, which means: the life of the one becomes the life of the other; their Existence is drawn from the actualization of life as communion, from life which is identified with self-offering love.

If, then, God is the true Existence and life, the cause and source and starting point of being, then in every case being, existence and life, is inseparable from the dynamic of love. Since the *mode* by which God *is* is love, and from this mode springs each possibility and expression of life, then life must function as love in order to be actualized. If it does not function as love, then existence does not constitute life. And this eventuality is a possibility of freedom of the person, since only the person can actualize life as love, and then only as an achievement of freedom. If the freedom of personal hypostases wishes to actualize existence not by the *mode* of life, the manner of the triadic fullness of life, but with another mode than that which constitutes life, then existence itself fails to achieve its *end* (goal) which is life. It fails in the very goal for which it exists; and then death appears as the last consequence of freedom in revolt.

The truth of the triadic God of the Church is not a particular "religious" truth, a better or worse answer than so many others that have been given to the problem of God. The truth of the triadic God is the Church's answer to life and death; it is the enlightenment of the mystery of existence, the revelation of the possibility for real life, free from time and decay.

6

The World

a. The scientific worldview

For the man who denies or rejects metaphysical questions, who does not trust the experience of the personal revelation of God, the world – material reality – often becomes a refuge or an alibi for his flight from the problem of God. He invokes the certainties of physics in order to prove the propositions of metaphysics to be uncertain and untrustworthy. He takes refuge in the clarity of *quantitative* measurements in order to escape the difficulty of the *qualitative* challenges which verify life.

Certainly, the knowledge of physical reality seems to be objective, directly verifiable, and accessible to every individual intellect. The data of physics are perceptible, tangible; they can be measured, expressed in mathematical relations, and interpreted logically. Historical experience, chiefly in the last two centuries, has shown that the human mind can subdue physical reality, can decipher its secrets, can require the forces of nature to serve the needs and desires of man, and to give his life comfort, convenience, enjoyment.

And so it has happened in our days that effective knowledge, "science" particularly, has been mythologized. Who can deny that man, without any aid, is exploring infinite space, and also the smallest atom of matter? With his strength he has abolished distance on our planet, he has tamed diseases, he has increased the average human life expectancy. And so man can easily swagger and believe that he can accomplish today thanks to "science" what before he tried vainly to achieve by prayers to God. Even if he has not yet solved all his problems, it is certain that, at the present rate of scientific progress, he will solve them shortly. Over-imaginative journalists in magazines for popular circulation cultivate this certainty in readers still more naïf, transferring to the omnipotence of "science" every problem and every unanswered human question. With enough money in America, you can already provide for the final abolition of death which science will achieve in a few years, remaining in the meantime frozen solid in preparation for coming back to life. Apart from anything else, this new impersonal divinity, this mythologized "science", is today the opium for the metaphysical enervation of the masses.

To be more precise, however, we must confess that the overvaluation of the capabilities of science and the search for supports for atheism in the area of physics was a symptom which exultantly manifested itself especially last century. Today though, the symptom survives not so much in the scientific workplace as at the level of the fantasy of the inexpert, those whom the commercial circuits exploit by preserving the myth of the omnipotence and of the wonder-working possibilities of "science".

In our century, it is precisely scientific progress which has come to enlighten the mystery of the world which surrounds us, to answer questions which have remained unanswered for centuries, but also to reveal the relative character of our knowledge, the minimal certainty of our "positive" sciences.

This is not the place to analyse at length this realization. Let us remember only that the new scientific conclusions which have arisen in our century demand that we desist from the certainty of knowledge which is assured by our senses or by the forms of our logic. This certainty was expressed chiefly by Euclidean geometry and Newtonian physics. Both of these have, though, been proved to be of limited capacity and inadequate to interpret the reality of the world. They are certainly useful if we are interpreting our limited sensible experience. But they are not valid either in the area of the largest or the smallest intervals.

The relativity which our scientific knowledge has in relation to the truth of the world was first shown with clarity by Albert Einstein. The two *theories of relativity* (special and general) showed that scientific observation can lead only to relative conclusions because the conclusions themselves are always a function of the position and motion of the observer. At the same time, Werner Heisenberg's *principle of indeterminacy* excluded definite prediction (consequently every deterministic eventuality) in the area of microphysics, and connected the result of scientific observation – not simply to the factor "observer" – but with the fact of observation itself, that is with each successive relationship of observer and observed. Similarly, the analysis of the phenomena of nuclear radiation by Max Planck and the quantum theory (quanta) of Niels Bohr demonstrated that the behavior of light can be identified with the composition or structure of the atom of matter, that is with a mode by which the smallest quantity of energy is presented to the observer. Appearing sometimes with the mode of the *particle* and sometimes in the mode of the *wave*, the smallest "unit" of matter or of light is an event of the transformation of energy. That means that the hypostasis if matter itself is energy, that matter contains the constituent properties of light, that light is the ideal matter.

b. The "logical" composition of matter

Philosophy was stopped for centuries at a time by the question, "What is matter?" One easy solution was to evade the question, to consider matter as self-evidently and always existing, or to say that God created it without explaining how the material emerged from the immaterial, the corruptible and transitory from the incorruptible and eternal. But in the case either of its self-existence or of its creation by God, matter remained equally unexplained. And it was really tragic to follow the disputes of materialists and idealists (disputes filled sometimes with blood), since the two supported an arbitrary metaphysical position giving it only a different name.

Before we arrived at the interpretations of contemporary physics, the only proposal within the history of philosophy which interprets the *composition* of matter was formulated by the Greek Fathers of the Church. St Gregory of Nyssa and St Maximus the Confessor saw matter as a fact of energy; they saw its composition as a *coincidence* and union of "logical qualities". The world in its entirety and in its every detail is an effected *word* (*lógos*), a personal creative activity of God. According to the account of Genesis, God created everything only by his word: "He spoke and it came to be" (Ps 33.9). The word of God does not come to an end, but is hypostasized in an effected event, "immediately becoming nature". As the human reason of a poet constitutes a new reality, which is the poem, outside of himself but at the same time a consequence and manifestation of his own reason, so also the word of God is given effect dynamically "in the ground and formation of creation".

To stay with this image: The poet's poem is a coincidence and union of words. In order for the poem to exist, the simple assembling of words is not enough, without their concurrence, their "shaping" or formation, their composition and structure. This concurrence of words which constitute the poem is a new reality of another "essence" from the "essence" of the poet, but nevertheless always revealing his own personal distinctiveness, and also unceasingly creative of new realizations of life. A poem is a word which effects and is effected dynamically within time, every reading of it is a new experiential unfolding, a different rational relationship, a beginning of new creative challenges.

Nothing of what constitutes a material body is not bodily, says Nyssa, not the shape, nor the colour, nor the weight, nor the density, nor the quantitative proportion, nor its dimensions, nor the dryness or wetness, nor its coolness or its heat, but all these are words which, when they concur and are gathered in unity, become matter. In the language of contemporary physics we would repeat the realization of Nyssa using simply a different terminology: We will refer to frequency of waves, to electro-magnetic fields, to nuclear radiation, to comparison of charges, that is to measurements of energy, to *words* yet again determinative of an effected event which is matter. The way to say what matter *is*, today is mathematics, that is the classification of properties in *logical* relations and of qualitative determinations in ratios of magnitude. Investigating the composition of matter, contemporary physics does not describe a given entity, but notes active conditions where they "emerge" in the challenge of experimentation. The variants of matter are summarized in the differentiation of categories of atoms of matter, and the atoms vary analogously to the combination of positive and negative electrical charges, that is they are expressions of only one fact of energy.

Whether we speak with the language of the Greek Fathers or with the language of contemporary physics, the reality of matter is an effected event accessible to man as a possibility of reason. Human reason meets in nature another reason; the knowledge of nature is only analogical or, better, dialogical. And reason is the characteristic of the person, the manifestation of an initial possibility of existence, before any other eventuality of hypostatic actualization. It is primordial and indescribable; it is personal self-consciousness, otherness and freedom in its self-revelation and its creative manifestation.

Within the limits of the world, man as a person meets God as a person. He meets him, not face to face, but hidden as he meets the poet hidden within the word of poetry and the artist within the word of colour. He is "the God who said, 'Let light shine out of darkness' ". But not even the disturbing conclusions of modern physics are enough for him to become truly known in his personal distinctiveness. Only "in our hearts" can "the light of the knowledge of God's glory" shine forth, and only then "in the face of Jesus Christ" (2 Cor 4.6). The name is the only possible revelation of the person, and the name of God has been given us in the historical person of Jesus – "the name above every name" – the glory and revelation of God the Father (Phil 2.9–11).

"The God who said, 'Let light shine out of darkness,' has shone in our hearts to give the light of the knowledge of God's glory in the face of Jesus Christ." God reveals God to us – he reveals himself by the light of a knowledge which is not a meaning or a concept, but a name and a person, Jesus Christ, the glory and revelation of God. The light of this knowledge occurs in our "hearts", in the depths of our personal identity, there where each of us is not his conduct, nor his character, nor his heredity or his psychology or his social mask, but only the identity of his *name*. There the name "Jesus" manifests the personal hypostasis of God, and the manifestation and revelation is principally an event of relationship, of adoption, of a call "out of not being into being" (Rm 4.17).

The God revealed in our hearts is he who has said that light is to shine from darkness, that from *non-being* is to be produced *being*, the first and ideal matter. His creative command becomes matter, a created energy, a bearer of his word – of the Word which even shines into our hearts the light of the knowledge of his Person. That first creative command, "Let there be light", contains every possibility for the created realization of what exists, the possibility of the existence of the world and of the existence of each of us, of our earthen vessels. But we meet this command which contains the meaning of the world and of its temporal beginning (even though it should be billions of years away from us) in the inmost core of our own personal existence, because there the personal bearer of this command is revealed, God the Word, Jesus.

The truth of the world is for the Church inseparable from the knowledge of God, and the knowledge of God inseparable from the person of Christ, and the person of Christ from the command of the Word at the beginning of time and in the depths of our hearts, inseparable from the light of the knowledge which raises us to life, to our adoption by God.

c. Natural energies

In the previous pages we have spoken about the Triadic God and about the way in which we can speak about his existence. We have distinguished the reality which is shown by the word "essence" or "nature" from the reality which is shown by the word "person" or "hypostasis". In speaking now about the world, we have used the word "energy", in order to show a third reality, which is distinguished both from "essence" and from "hypostasis" and which is just as constitutive of what exists as the other two and at the same time their consequence.

In fact, the Theology of the Church interprets the reality of existence, the appearance and disclosure of *being*, starting from these two fundamental distinctions: It distinguishes essence or nature from the person or hypostasis, as it distinguishes the energies both from the nature and from the hypostasis. In these three basic categories, nature – hypostasis – energies, Theology summarizes the *mode of existence* of God, the world, and man.

But what exactly do we designate with the word *energies*? We designate those potentials of nature or essence to make known the hypostasis and its existence, to make it known and participable. This definition will be more clear if we again use an example from our immediate experience, if we speak about the energies of human nature or our essence.

Every man has understanding, reason, will, desire, imagination; every man works, loves, creates. All these capacities, and still others analogous to them, are common to all people and therefore we say that they belong to the human nature or essence. They are natural capacities or energies which differentiate man from every other being.

But these natural energies, while they are common to every man, are disclosed and actualized by each man in a unique way, distinct and unrepeatable. All men have understanding, will, desire, imagination; but every particular man thinks, wills, desires, imagines in a manner absolutely different. Therefore we say that the natural energies not only differentiate man from every other being, but also are manifested in a way that differentiates every man from all his fellow men. The natural energies are the way in which the otherness of each human hypostasis, that is of every human person, is revealed and disclosed.

There is no other way for us to know the personal otherness of man, than by the manifestation of natural energies. The natural energies permit us to know the otherness of the person by *sharing* in the way or in the *how* of their manifestation. The way or the how the word of Kavafi differs from the word of Sepheris, the love of our father from the affection of our mother, is something that cannot be designated objectively, except with conditional expressions and comparative images.

In order for us to *know* this difference, we must share, to have
the experience of sharing, in the word or in the love of the
other person. We have said in some preceding pages that for us
to know a person we must have a relationship with him. Now
to complete this concept we can say that the relationship does
not mean a simple meeting, a direct view or observation, but a
sharing or participation in the energies which reveal the
otherness of the person in his facial expression, in his word, in
his loving manifestation, etc.

St Maximus the Confessor made a very significant observation on this subject. He realized that there are two kinds of
energies: those homogeneous and those heterogeneous to the
nature of the one giving effect to the energies, as he
characterized them. There are, that is, energies which are
manifested in a manner homogeneous (of the same kind, of
the same character, of the same quality) with the nature of the
one acting. There are also energies which are revealed by
means of essences of a kind different from the nature of the
one acting. The human voice, for instance, articulate expression, is an energy of reason homogeneous with the nature of
man. But it can also be a disclosure of the energy of the reason
by means of essences "heterogeneous" to the nature of man
and the ability of other essences to be formed into reason, such
as writing, colour, marble, music.

And so we are able to understand how it is possible for us to
know a person both directly and indirectly: We know him
directly when we meet him, we hear his word, we see his
expression, his look, his laugh, when we love him and he loves
us. But we also know a person indirectly when we just read
what he has written, when we hear the music which he has
composed or we see the pictures which he has drawn.

And in both cases the knowledge is incomparably fuller than
any "objective" informing of us about a person. Perhaps we
can bring together all the information that there is about the
life, say, of Van Gogh, we can read all his biographies which
have been written. But we know the person of Van Gogh,
what is unique, distinct and unrepeatable in his existence, only
when we see his paintings. There we meet a reason (*lógos*)
which is his only and we separate him from every other

painter. When we have seen enough pictures by Van Gogh and then encounter one more, then we say right away: This *is* Van Gogh. We distinguish immediately the otherness of his personal reason, the uniqueness of his creative expression.

Nevertheless, even this acquaintance with the person of Van Gogh by means of the study of his work, even though it is incomparably fuller than the biographical information about his person, does not cease to be an indirect knowledge. It would be direct knowledge if we met Van Gogh himself, spoke with him and lived with him, loved him and were loved by him. But here, we wish to insist on the possibility which exists, to know a person by the revelation of his reason (his existential otherness) by means of essences heterogeneous to the essence of his own person. Van Gogh is a man according to his essence, while one of his pictures is canvas and colours according to its essence. But these colours on top of canvas become a *word* which reveals the "secret" of the person, the uniqueness and distinctiveness of Van Gogh's existence. The creative *energy* of Van Gogh, his artistic creation, makes possible our own sharing and participation in the knowledge of his person.

A further observation from the same example: All of us who recognize the uniqueness of the word of Van Gogh facing one of his pictures, share, each of us, in this word in a personal way, that is unique, distinct and unrepeatable. Nor does the personal sharing of each of us "cut" the word which reveals the otherness of Van Gogh into as many parts as there are people sharing in this word by means of the picture. Personally uttered, the word remains simple and undivided while, at the same time, "it is shared with all in a singular way." The painted picture (like the poem, the statue, the music, the human voice) represents the energy of a man's reason (*lógos*), that is, the possibility for us to share in the knowledge of the personal otherness of the man – for all of us to share who see the same picture in the same otherness of the one person.

d. Natural theory

Perhaps we can now understand more fully what exactly the Church means when it defines that the world is a result of the Energies of God, a revelation of the creative *word* of God (of the Person of God the Word) by essences "heterogeneous" to the Essence of God. The material reality of the world and the endless number of species or essences which give form to this reality are a result of the free personal creative energy of God. The world is essentially (by its essence) different from God, while it is at the same time a word which reveals the personal otherness of God.

The Fathers of the Church term the study of the word of God within nature *natural theory*, the discovery of His personal otherness within each small feature of beauty and of wisdom of the world. The matter itself of the world is an event dynamically effected, an energy "heterogeneous" to the Nature of God. And we distinguish the created energy of God which constitutes the world from his uncreated Energies, which are "heterogeneous" to created things and "homogeneous" to God – Energies which we term with a common name "grace" or God's gift of life to man.

We know the Person of God indirectly by studying the reality of the world, the otherness of the word of created divine energies which constitute and compose the natural universe. And we come to know the Person of God directly by means of the uncreated Energies by which God "is shared entirely" and "is shared with all in a singular way" remaining simple and undivided, offering to the participant what He has "by nature" except his "essential identity", and raising man, in the words of Scripture, "to share in the divine nature" (2 Pt 1.4).

e. "Mediator" – "microcosm"

But for the Church, the existence and truth of the world do not represent, plainly and simply, a possibility of indirect knowledge of God by man. The "end" and the purpose of the world are not only indirect. When we say in the Church that the matter of the world is energy and that the universe is an event dynamically effected, we presuppose an "end" or purpose for which the event of the world has been effected.

At least, for the Greek Fathers of the Church the reality of the world is an energy since the world is created, it is a creation, a work, of God. And something that is created is, for the Fathers, a being which has its cause and its purpose outside of itself – in contradistinction with the *uncreated* existence of God which is both cause and purpose of itself (and only this constitutes absolute and unlimited being).

When we say that created beings have the cause and the purpose of their existence outside of themselves, we mean to express this: that God has created beings (He is himself their cause) and that he has created them for a purpose. The nature of beings is *active*, because existence itself tends toward something which is not simply the fact that they exist, but the realization of a purpose for which they exist.

From the revelation of God in history and in the Bible, the Fathers inferred the purpose for which God had created everything: that all beings share in the life of God, that they form the "glory", that is the manifestation of God, so that God would be "all in all" (1 Cor 11.28). With the limited capacities of our language, we say that God is the fullness of existence and of life, and he wishes that all that exists participate in this fullness, that every existing thing be an expression of divine life, a participation in the community of love which constitutes the mode of existence of God, the Being of God.

But the effected event of the world is not led automatically to the purpose or "end" of sharing in the life of God – the energy which constitutes the matter of the world is not an autonomous and self-powered course to existential fullness. The insertion of the nature of what is created into the life of the uncreated cannot be a result of necessity, but an event of freedom. And the only created existence who can realize life as freedom is man. Therefore the Holy Scripture, like its patristic interpretation, sees in man the "intermediary" (acting as an intermediary or mediating) for the reality of the existential "end" and purpose of the whole creation. Human freedom is interposed in the nature of the created like a wedge of possibility between the given and the intended, between existence and the "end" of existence.

In the language of the Church, man is the *priest* of the whole creation of God, the one who has the possibility to relate and to offer to God created nature, to enthrone on the throne of Divinity the "mud" of the earth. Often in the Fathers we find the expression that man is a *microcosm*: As a natural construction he sums up the elements of the whole world. But these elements after the *fall* of man, his alteration "against nature" (as we shall see in a following chapter), are found within him and in the world around him in a state of fragmentation and division. Remaining, though, a personal existence even after his fall, a rational psychosomatic hypostasis, man retains the possibility of realizing dynamically in his person the unity of the world, to sum up the word (*lógos*) of the world in a personal reply to the call of God for the communion and relationship of the created with the uncreated, to manifest the general word (*lógos*) of the world as a personal word of glorification of the creator by the creation, to give to the energy which constitutes the world the right direction and drive toward its existential end. Therefore according to the word of Scripture, "the creation waits with eager longing for the revealing of the sons of God … because the creation itself will be set free from its bondage to decay and obtain the glorious liberty of the children of God. We know that the whole creation has been groaning in travail together until now" (Rom 8.19, 21-22 *RSV*).

In our days, a mistaken religious upbringing has led many people to consider the Church as a means or instrument to ensure individual salvation for each of us – and when they talk of "salvation" they mean an unlimited kind of survival after death in some "other" world. But in reality the Church entrusts to everyone the enormous honour to be responsible for the salvation of the whole world, of this world whose flesh is our flesh and whose life is our life. And *salvation* for the Church is the liberation of life from corruption and death, the transformation of survival into existential fullness, the sharing of the created in the mode of life of the uncreated.

f. Ascetical apprenticeship

The Church's truth concerning the world is not a theoretical position, an abstract theorizing, a "dogmatic" interpretation of reality. It is a knowledge which is won dynamically, an achievement of a relationship with the world. Man cannot attain the truth of the world as long as he confronts the data of physical reality as neutral objects, useful for the satisfaction of his own needs and desires. If we narrow ourselves to this confident and utilitarian interpretation of the world, it is possible that we will develop our "positive" sciences and their technological applications to an amazing degree. But the world will remain for us an irrational given, a simple appearance swinging in a vacuum or in nothingness.

Every true art surpasses the "objective" encounter with the world. An artist, for instance, seeks to impress on his pictures the uniqueness which an object, a person or place, possesses in his eyes. From the sensible impression he erects and represents his own unique and unrepeatable relationship with the things. He is not interested in the photographic impression of reality – then he would be a "positive scientist" and not a painter. He is a painter, because he succeeds in discovering, even in the most trivial objects of everyday use, the "splendour" in the uniqueness of a *word* which addresses him personally. And the acceptance of this word is another personal word: the unique and unrepeatable representative expression of the painter.

That encounter with and study of the world is the beginning of another step which the Church calls *asceticism*. Ascetism is the struggle to renounce my egocentric tendency to see everything as neutral objects, subject to my needs and desires. By poverty and submission to the common rules of asceticism, I fight precisely against my egocentric claim, I transpose the axis of my life from my ego to my relationship with the world which surrounds me, because the relationship begins only when in practice I desist from the tendency to subject everything. Then I begin to respect what surrounds me, to discover that it is not simply objective impersonal riches (of objective utility), but *things*, that is, results of activity, what has been done by a creative Person. I discover the personal character of the data of the world, a uniqueness of reason in each something, a possibility of relationship, a ground of loving reference to God. My relationship with the world becomes then an indirect relationship with God, the maker of the world, and the practical use of the world a ceaseless study of the truth of the world, a constantly deeper knowledge inaccessible to "positive" science.

I will venture another example: A trifling object of everyday use – a pen, a pencil – passes from my hands indifferently, I use it without giving it special meaning, and if I lose it, I replace it without a second thought. But if this same trifling object happens to be a memento for me, as we might say, if it is a gift which some beloved person has given me, then its value for me is as great even as my love for him of whom it reminds me. Every time that I use it, I not only exploit its usefulness, but it is as if I accept the aid which it offers me straight from the person whom I love. And so, an object neutral in other respects becomes an event of relationship, a ground for a bond and personal reference, an endless re-confirmation of love. But this example is, nevertheless, inadequate, because the world is not simply a gift or memento of God to man, but a dynamically effected polyphony of words which incarnate divine love in an hypostasis of creation, while at the same time calling human freedom to co-ordinate the created polyphony in affirmation and reception of the divine love.

g. Use of the world

The ecclesial cosmology which is studied in practice by asceticism can be the general mode of life and use of the world. And this not only in the core or the "leaven" of the eucharistic community, but in the widest dimensions of a social whole in any historical period. It can constitute, that is, an expression of a human culture, an expression of art and technology and economy and politics which respects the world, which uses it as a gift of love, and which studies the principle of the uniqueness of things, such as the possibility for matter to incarnate the relationship of man with God, to share in the life of the uncreated.

Such a culture certainly flourished in the so-called byzantine and post-byzantine period of Hellenism. Here is not the place to show how the administrative institutions in Byzantium both in justice and the organization of the economy and the private dealings expressed the ecclesial cosmology in the activity of life. A lot has been written about it, and it would be enough for someone to study just the architecture of a byzantine church or even the technique of fitting the stones. Thus he would there touch directly the ethos of this culture, the way people respected and studied the inner principle of the material, not forcing the material to make it obey the purpose which his own understanding has conceived. Using the materials of the world, he is trained in self-denial and the renunciation of his egocentric vanity; he lifts up the possibilities which the material itself possesses to be "rationalized", to form a "dialogue" with the craftsman – a dialogue which no rationalistic technique can repeat.

Today we live in a culture which is found at the antipodes of byzantine culture, and therefore it is almost impossible for us to follow the ethos of that use of the world and of the truth which dictated it. Today our relationship with the world is becoming more and more an indirect relationship – the machine intervenes to subordinate nature and her forces to the demands of understanding, negating the resistance which the material can offer to the efficiency of our own programming. This individual authority over nature is perfectly self-evident to us – and therefore it also passes into our character or ethos: Turning or pushing a button we have light, heat, coolness, transportation, telecommunications and a host of other direct results. There is nothing bad in all this, all are desirable and respectable products, they make the life of man easier, they reduce the toil which survival formerly demanded. But they also free the insatiable egocentric voracity of man, his instinctive tendency to have, to consume and to rejoice sensually, without limits or barriers.

Nevertheless, this individualistic imposition on the world that technology secures for us today, is in practice the application of a cosmology which accepts nature as an impersonal and neutral given at the service of the wishes and needs of man. There is not the least suspicion about a personal relationship with the world, with the reality of life as an event of communion and relationship. But the practical application of so radically anti-christian a cosmology is proved to be plainly opposed to life, a direct threat of death for nature and man. Today, we call this threat pollution of the natural environment, exhaustion of the sources of energy, disease-producing food. The poisoned atmosphere of the large cities, the foul water, the dead soil, the disease-producing pesticides, and whatever other nightmarish symptoms contemporary man lives in industrial communities, all prove the tragic mistake in his relationship with the world, a mistake which is rapidly taking on the dimensions of a deadly threat. What we have called "progress" and "development", has proved to be a rape of nature and her corruption, which is ineluctably a torment and threat of death for man.

The need for us to study with respect and humility the truth of the world, to find again our true relationship with it, is today – and for the first time in the history of man – a problem, literally, of life and death.

7

Man

a. Image

In the Tradition of the undivided Church and its historical continuity in Orthodoxy, we learn the truth about man by studying the revelation of the truth about God. Therefore, since a descriptive anthropology is not enough for us (one which the "human sciences", as they are called today, can give us), we look rather for an interpretation of the fact of human existence, the illumination of those aspects of human being which remain inaccessible to objective explanation.

From the written tradition of the revelation of God, the Holy Scripture of the Church, God is affirmed as a personal Existence, and man is created *in the image* of God. Man is himself also a personal existence, even though he is a created nature. This initial relationship of man with God, which constitutes the very mode by which man exists, is pictured in the first pages of the Old Testament, in a poetic and symbolic narrative, from which Christian thought has always drawn the fundamental presuppositions of ecclesial anthropology.

We read, then, in the book of Genesis, that God fashioned the world in six days. God created everything that forms the world with just the command of his word. On the sixth day, the same day that he completed the creation by calling into existence the wild animals, the cattle, and the reptiles of the earth, when God saw the beauty of the whole creation, he proceeded to fashion man. With its figurative language the biblical narrative marks a distinct activity of God to create man. It is no longer the creative command, but the special expression of a decision of God – in which Christian hermeneutics (as we have seen in previous pages) has always distinguished the first revelation of God as Trinity: "Let us make man in our own image and likeness, and let them rule the fish of the sea and the birds of the sky and the cattle and all the earth and all the reptiles which creep on the earth" (Gen 1.26).

It is not a question here any longer of one more of the creatures which make up the world, but of a creature which the will of God distinguishes from all the others in order for it to be an *image* of God within the world – which means an immediate revelation, appearance, or representation of God. [1] Therefore, man *rules* within creation, not in the sense of an endowed overseer or imposed master, but in the sense of the guide who directs the whole creation to its final *reason* (*lógos*) or purpose.

The expression of this special will and decision of God to create man is accomplished in the biblical image by a separate act of God: "God formed man, dust from the earth, and he breathed in his face a breath of life, and man became a living soul" (Gen 2.7). God "fashioned" no other creature in the biblical narrative. The material to fashion man is nothing other than the dust of the earth – and this property of the earthly will even be the name of the first man: Adam (= of the earth). But earthly human nature is constructed by a separate divine activity, he is "fashioned" by God in order to receive in the sequel the inspiration of the breath of God and for man to be raised to be a "living soul".

To breath in the face of someone else was always for the Hebrews (and for the Semitic peoples generally) an act of the deepest sybolism: it means that you transmit to the other your breath, something very inwardly yours, your own self-consciousness or your spirit. This is so since breathing is a presupposition of life, the element which consititutes you as an active being, and all the experiences – fear, anger, joy, pride – all influence breathing, they show a relationship of breathing with your deepest being, your own self. When, then, the

[1] By the word *icon* (image), the seventy translators of the OT translated into Greek the Hebrew term *tselem*, which means precisely, "appearance", "representation". "equivalence", "substitute'

Scripture says that God blew his own breath in the earthly face of man, this image is to demonstrate the communication to man of certain marks of the very existence of God. In biblical language the result of this communication is that man becomes a *living soul*.

b. Soul

The word *soul* is among the most difficult words in the Bible and in Christian literature. Moreover, confusion was added to the meaning of the word, since the Greeks used it with a different meaning. Today, most people, almost self-evidently, understand the word "soul" more with the ancient Greek (particularly Platonic) and less with its biblical meaning. They believe that, as there exists within the body of man blood, lymph, bone marrow, in the same way there exists an immaterial element, spiritual, essentially different from our material composition and precisely this is the soul – something transparent and indefinte, which leaves us with the last breath when we die and goes "somewhere else".

But this is not the biblical meaning of the word. The seventy translators of the Old Testament carried over into Greek with the word *psyche* ("soul") the Hebrew *nephesh*, a term with many meanings. Anything which has life is called a soul, every animal, but more commonly within Scripture it pertains to man. It signifies the way in which life is manifested in man. It does not refer just to one department of human existence – the spiritual, in opposition to the material – but signifies the whole man, as a single living hypostasis. The soul does not merely dwell in the body, but is expressed by the body, which itself, like the *flesh* or *heart*, corresponds to our ego, to the way in which we realize life. A man is a soul, he is someone, since this constitutes the sign of life, as much an external manifestation as interiority and subjectivity. But if the soul is the sign of life, it does not signify that it is also the source or cause of life, as the Greeks believed. It is, rather, the bearer of life, and therefore it is often identified in the Old Testament only with the manifestation of life on earth (the soul dies, it is handed over to death, but it also is raised, when life returns to the dead body), while in the New Testament it appears also as a bearer of *eternal life*, and therefore the *salvation of the soul* is identified with the possibility of life which does not know corruption and death.

The Fathers of the Christian Church interpreting the Scripture respected absolutely the very important meaning of the word "soul" and did not try to define it with only one interpretation. They saw both in the soul and in the body of man two differentiated and often co-inhering modes by which the image of God in man is revealed. But they refused to schematize the content of the "image" in a particular definition; they sought to preserve the mystery of the mode of the divine Existence and its imprinting on human existence from the danger of intellectual schematization.

Much later, chiefly in the middle ages and afterwards and especially in the European West, when Christian theology began to succumb to the temptation of intellectual schematization, the "image" was interpreted with "objective" categories; it was identified with particular properties which characterize the "spiritual nature" of man. The most general understanding of man received in the West a strong influence from ancient Greek thought, with, though, exaggerated simplifications. The Greek definition of man as an "animal having reason" (*animal rationale* as it was put in the West) was interpreted in the form of a real, antithetical distinction of soul and body, matter and spirit. Man was thought of as, in principal, a biological being endowed additionally with a soul or with a soul and spirit.

Within the scheme of this opposition, the "image" was limited to one of these two "parts" of the nature of man, the spiritual "part", that is, the soul – since the bodily, material "part" is by definition unable to represent the immaterial and spiritual God. The soul, then, of man – each one's individual soul – was endowed with three properties which characterize God himself, and therefore impart His image to man: *rationality*, *free will*, and *dominion*.

c. Rationality – free will – dominion

Not to torment the reader with extensive analyses, we will note only this: These three attributes were used as well by the Greek Fathers to interpret the "image", but chiefly in the attempt to determine the mode of existence of the entire man, without fragmenting and division of his nature into "parts". Rationality, free will, and dominion are not simply "mental" or "spiritual" qualities, but a concise recapitulation of the mode in which man exists as personal otherness – which is particularly an otherness as to nature: Even if the nature of man is created, he has been endowed with the possibility of a mode of existence which is other than, different from, the mode of existence of the created. He is endowed with the possibility of the mode of divine existence, which is manifested especially in the gift of rationality, of free will, and of dominion. But these gifts reveal, without exhausting it, the image of God in man, and therefore the disturbance of their functions does not take away the mode of personal existence with which the nature of man has been endowed.

This formulation may seem theoretical, but the reader will grasp its significance if we adopt the contrasting version which western people have accepted: If we agree that rationality, free will, and dominion define and exhaust the image as given qualities of man's soul or "spiritual nature", then the consequences are literally inhuman. It will, then, be necessary in any situation of mental illness or of traumatic damage to the brain which entails an upset or loss of rationality, free will, and dominion to demote the man from the status of an image of God to the level of a simple animal. And when he is from birth burdened with such a loss, he is not to be considered a human existence.

The Christian West was led to such ultimately inescapable theories (we will see below the other inescapable confusion which the teaching of the West has invoked for the *absolute destiny* of man), since in its spiritual environment it has de-emphasized and progressively ignored the truth of the person, which is a fundamental presupposition in order to approach Christian revelation. And the loss of the truth of the person is not the result of accidental co-incidences, attitudes of mind, or currents and tendencies which have been cultivated in the West – such as intellectualism and the demand for "objective" certainties. All these are consequences, basically, of an *ethical* failure, of the inability of westerners, for some time past, to exist and to express themselves *ecclesially*, that is, to realize life and the expression of life as an event of communion. They have separated the Church from the triadic mode of existence; they have changed it into a "religion" which each one accepts individually and to whose dogmas, organization and rules he decides to submit himself as an individual. Thus life and truth are transformed from an event of relationship and communion into an anthropocentric subjectivism. The truth has become a knowledge subject to the conceptual demands of the subject and life, likewise, a subjective realization of utilitarian goals. God himself has been understood as an absolute Subject (with which understanding man has transformed him into an object, transcendent certainly, but subject to the rules of correct reasoning). God owes his existence to his given Essence, while the Persons of the triadic revelation function simply as modes (*modi*) of activity or as "internal relationships" of the Essence, seeing that a unique character is attributed – as is logically necessary – to this objectified Subject. And when both God and man are understood as subjects or individuals, as beings in themselves beyond any dynamic relationship or communion, then the one "images" the other with objectively given qualitative analogies. We refer to the absolute and we attribute to God the marks which characterize the human subject – and finally God is even created "in the image and likeness" of man, instead of the other way.

d. Person

We might dare to summarize the orthodox ecclesial interpretation of the "image" in the following formulation: Man has been endowed by God with the gift of being a person, with personhood, which is to exist in the same mode in which God exists. What constitutes the divinity of God is His personal Existence, the Trinity of Personal Hypostases which make up the divine Being, the diving Nature or Essence, in a life of love, which is a life of freedom from any necessity.

God is God since he is a Person, that is since his Existence does not depend on anything, not even his Nature or Essence. As a Person – that is freely – he constitutes his Essence or Nature; it is not his Nature or Essence which makes his Existence obligatory. He exists, since he freely *wills* to exist, and this willing is actualized as love, as a triadic communion. Therefore, God *is* love (1 Jn 4.16), his own Being is love.

And God has imprinted this same possiblity of *personal* existence on human nature. Human nature is created, a given; it is not the personal freedom of man which constitutes his *being*, which makes up his essence or nature. But this created nature exists only as a *personal* hypostasis of life; each one is a *personal* existence which can hypostasize life as love, that is as freedom from the limitations of his created nature, as freedom from every necessity – just like the uncreated God.

Still more schematically: God is a Nature and three Persons; man is a nature and "innumerable" persons. God is consubstantial and in three hypostases, man is consubstantial and in innumerable hypostases. The difference of natures, the difference of uncreated and created, can be transcended at the level of the common mode of existence, the mode of personal existence – and this truth has been revealed to us by the incarnation of God, by the Person of Jesus Christ. For man to be an image of God means that each one can realize his existence as Christ realizes life as love, as freedom and not as natural necessity. Each can realize his existence as a person, like the Persons of the triadic Divinity. Consequently, man can realize his existence as eternity and incorruptibility, just as the divine life of triadic co-inherence and communion is eternal and incorruptible.

e. Scientific language

The reader who feels uncomfortable with this terminology of "nature", "person", "hypostasis", might perhaps demand answers to more specific questions: If man is an image of God, how is this image revealed in his body and how in his soul or spirit? What becomes of the image of God in man when the body dies and decomposes in the earth? Is every trace of his soul or spirit extinguished together with the last look or smile?

These are serious questions and, if they are not answered, everything remains up in the air and illusive. But the reader must understand that the language needed to answer such questions cannot be the language of physics and geometry, the language of mass, quantities, and measures of size. But another language is needed, one able to articulate experiences of qualitative differentiation, experiences or relationship, and sensitivities which reveal a knowledge which the senses do not assure. The Church talks about these subjects with such a language, which was largely borrowed from the dramatic, age-long struggle of Greek philosophy for the meaning of life and existence; only, the ecclesial language did not remain intellectualistically philosophical, but became as well a song, a hymn, a worship, an action, that is, of communion and celebration. Here we retain only the philosophical shell of this language; but we emphasize that the reader will find the fullness of the "semantics" in the ecclesial act of worship, in the experience of communion of the ecclesial body.

The question is then: What happens to the image of God in man, when the body dies and every expression of the soul is lost? We must see if there are words especially to say what the body is, what the soul or spirit is, and which of the two constitutes what we call the existence of man, his personal identity, ego, or self-consciousness.

Contemporary rationalist man has the tendency to identify human existence – the ego, identity, the soul, self-consciousness, the spirit – with the concrete and tangible object which is the biological organism of man and its various functions. Everything depends on the function of the brain "centres", and the manner of functioning of these centres is rigidly predetermined by their biochemical composition, or by the also biochemical genetic foundation of the individual, the chromosomes – DNA – which contain the "code" for the development of the personality. There is, then, no room left

over for us to assume the existence of a soul nor, consequently, the possibility for "something" of man to survive
after the death of his biological organism.

But unfortunately this so simplified version – even if it is
very widely circulated today and so comfortably trusted –
leaves huge gaps in the interpretation of man, at least as many
as the "immortality of the soul" of popularized platonism. In
principle, the science of biochemistry, and of every true
science, is only able to discover and describe, even in its most
concrete analytical determinations. It notes, for instance, that
the possibilities for the development of the organism are
contained in the "code" of the primitive chromosomes; it
ascertains the organic unity within which the function of the
cerebal centres, etc, operate. But it will go beyond its limits as a
strict science, if it proceeds to formulate unproved metaphysical conclusions and claim that the biochemical composition of
the chromosomes and the function of the particular organs or
organic "centres" of man's biological organism do not simply
effect and reveal, but that they both ground and constitute the
mode of hypostatic otherness of each human person.

But why should we exclude that what each man *is* as a
unique, distinct and unrepeatable personal existence is owed
exclusively and only to the differentiation of the biochemical
composition of its chromosomes and by extension to the
function of the various "centres" of its brain? Why do we
restrict the rôle of biochemical composition and biological
functions solely to the *activity* and *manifestation* of the hypostatic
otherness of each man, and not extend it also to its foundation
and composition?

For the simple reason that such an extension is excluded by
the logic of scientific methodology itself today. If we agree
that the biochemical composition of the chromosomes and the
function of the cerebral "centres" do not simply effect and
reveal, but are the cause of hypostatic otherness of each man,
then we agree that his hypostatic otherness (or personality, or
psychology, or identity, the ego) of man is determined with a
strict regulation by the biological organism and its functions.
We agree, that is, that the biological formations and functions
which comprise and maintain the corporeality of man define

and exhaust by themselves all the existential fact or hypostasis of the human subject and, consequently, no "psychogenic" factor may restrict or restrain the autonomy of these functions.

But such a claim is upset by just one very small example from the field of another "positive" science, today's clinical psychology. An anorexic child drives itself to death, proving that its "soul" is determinative of its existence or hypostasis incomparably more than the rhythmical mechanism of its biological functions. And in its more positivistic versions, the contemporary science of psychology and psychoanalysis proves in short order – with a mass of revealing examples like the anorexic child – that what we call subjectivity or ego precedes and determines the function of the biological corporeality. If, in spite of all this, we want to insist that even the psychogenic anorexia of the child has its cause in biochemical reactions, then we ought to demonstrate the reasons by which the biological factor is able in this case to kill itself – for the biological factor to oppose the biological factor. And it is not possible for an internally consistent scientific logic to adopt reasons which account for such a contradiction.

f. Ecclesial language

Biblical and ecclesial anthropology are not opposed to the discoveries or language which contemporary biology uses, nor is it undermined by it. It is just that it troubles the partisans of that popularized platonism which has often been dressed in Christian garb (especially in the West) and which has sought to supplant the Church's truth concerning man.

In fact, if we agree that the human body is an entity in itself and the human soul another entity in itself, that only the latter (the soul) constitutes man, and that by itself it comprises the personality, the ego, the identity of the subject – while the body is just a shell or the instrument of the soul which only indirectly influences the soul – then certainly contemporary biology would hold many objections to our interpretation and its language would be incompatible with ours.

But such a platonizing interpretation does not find support in the biblical and patristic tradition. We will answer the question, "What is the body and what is the soul of man?" with the criteria of the ecclesial tradition: Both the body and the soul are energies of human nature, that is the modes by which the event of the hypostasis (or personality, the ego, the identity of the subject) is given effect. What each specific man *is*, his real existence or his hypostasis, this inmost *I* which constitutes him as an existential event, is identified neither with the body nor with the soul. The soul and the body only reveal and disclose what man *is*; they form energies, manifestation, expressions, functions to reveal the hypostasis of man.

Let us recall here what we have said about the energies in the last chapter. They are common properties of the nature of man which nevertheless effect and express the unique, distinct and unrepeatable character of each specific human hypostasis. All of us have the same functions bodily and mental: breathing, digestion, metabolism, understanding, judgment, imagination – but these common functions differentiate definitively every human subject. Its bodily and mental functions differentiate it, as much its purely bodily or spiritual characteristics (such as its finger prints or its feelings of inferiority), as their co-inherence (the look, reason, physiognomy, gestures) – all those ways of subjective expression which make it difficult for us to distinguish the boundaries between the soul and the body.

What man *is*, then, his hypostasis, cannot be identified either with his body or with his soul. It is only *given effect*, expressed and revealed by its bodily or spiritual functions. Therefore, no bodily infirmity, injury or deformity and no mental illness, loss of the power of speech or dementia can touch the truth of any man, the inmost *I* which constitutes him as an existential event.

Furthermore, even for our direct experience what we call body is not a determinate given, an unchangeable being, but a dynamically effected event, a complex of unceasingly effected functions (and in the discovery and description of biochemical unions, mechanisms, developments which constitute these functions, we could adopt with no difficulty the

results of contemporary biology or their eventual improvements and changes in the future). And what we call soul is also
a dynamically effected event, a complex of ceaselessly
effected functions which reveal and express the living existence of man. We give different names to these functions: we
speak of reason, imagination, judgment, creativity, ability to
love, etc. just as we speak of conscious, subconscious,
unconscious. In the ascertainment and description of these
functions, we can adopt with no difficulty the results and
language of contemporary psychology and psychoanalysis or
their eventual future improvements – always assuming respect
for the boundaries of science and recognizing its investigative
and descriptive character. And so, with whatever language we
express it, we could formulate the conclusion that the biolog-
ical-bodily as much as the psychological individuality of man
is not, but *is being* completed dynamically. It is completed with
progressive development and, after weakening and debility,
with death, the final "effacing" of the psychosomatic energies. But, what man *is* remains untouched by this process of
development, maturity, old age, and death.

For the Church and her truth, what man *is* as a personal
existence "before" God, that is what constitutes the image of
God in man, cannot be immobilized in some temporal moment
or period. The infant who "does not understand" and the
mature man at the peak of his psychosomatic powers and the
one sunk in the incapacity of old age or even senility are the
same person before God. Since what constitutes man as an
hypostasis, what gives him an ego and identity is not psychosomatic functions, but his relationship with God, the fact that
God loves him with an erotic singularity that calls into
existence what does not exist (Rm 4.17), establishing and
founding the personal otherness of man. Man is a person, an
image of God, since he exists as a possibility of responding to
the erotic call of God. With his psychosomatic functions, man
"administers" this possibility; he answers positively or nega-
tively to the call of God guiding his existence either to life,
which is the relationship with, or to death, which is the
separation from, God.

The call of God, which establishes the personal hypostasis of man, is not altered or changed according to the integrity of the psychosomatic functions. Nor is it influenced by the scientific interpretations of the progress or evolution of this integrity. The intervention of God's call constitutes man and therefore the Church is not upset nor is her truth under attack, if science accepts the "evolution of the species" and it is proved that man is descended biologically from the ape. Man's difference from the ape is not founded on quantitative differentiation of the completeness of the psychosomatic functions, but in the qualitative differentiation, in the fact that man "administers" with his psychosomatic functions – whether he admits it or not – his existential response to the invitation to life which God directs to him. The biblical image of the formation of man by God and the breathing of the divine breath into the human person shows, however, not the biological creation, but certainly the beginning of personal self-consciousness and identity and freedom and self-control. If this beginning is joined to the biological appearance of the human species or if it is interjected in some link of consecutive evolution of the species, the truth of the biblical and ecclesial anthropology will not change.

g. Life after death

From all this, perhaps the Church's faith in the immortality of man is illuminated, the faith in "life after death". Many religions and philosophies proclaim the "immortality of the soul", but the Church is differentiated from all these, because she understands immortality, not as an uninterpreted form of "survival" after death, but as a transcendence of death by means of the relationship with God. Death is, for the Church, separation from God, the denial of the relationship with Him, the refusal of life as love and erotic communion. How is man by himself, with his own existential capacities which are created (they contain neither their cause nor their goal), able to survive eternally? When all the psychosomatic functions are extinguished with the last breath, the created nature of man has exhausted at last its own possibilities for survival.

The Church's faith in the eternity of man is not the conviction that there is somehow a future "condition" where "something" from man survives, his "soul" or his "spirit". But it is the certainty that my nature and its existential possibilities do not secure the hypostasis of my life; my relationship with God, his erotic love for me, secure it and constitute it. Faith in eternity is the trust that this love will not stop but will always constitute my life whether my psycho-somatic capacities function or do not function.

Faith in *eternal life* is not an ideological certainty; it is not defended with arguments. It is a motion of trust, a deposit of our hopes and our thirst for life in the love of God. He who gives us here and now such a wealth of life, in spite of our own psychosomatic resistances to the realization of life (of real life which is a loving self-transcendence and communion), he has promised us also fullness of life, direct adoption, a face to face relationship with Him, when the last resistances of our rebellion are put out in the earth.

How this new relationship with Him will operate, by means of what functions, I do not know. I merely rely on it. What I do know from such revelation of truth as he has given us is that the relationship will always be personal, that before him, I will be me, as God knows me and loves me, I will *be* with my name and with the possibility of dialogue with Him, like Moses or Elijah on Mt Tabor. That is enough; perhaps it is more than enough.

h. The distinction between the sexes

In the biblical narrative of man's creation, the truth of the image of God which is imprinted in man is followed or fulfilled with the distinction of the sexes, the differentiation of man and woman. "And God made man; in the image of God he made him; male and female he made them" (Gen 1.27). In this phrase, ecclesial hermeneutics saw the joining of the "image" with the "power of love" of man, the power which drives him to realize life as communion with the other sex, while at the same time this same force is also constitutive of life; it is the *way* for human life to be constituted in new personal hypostases and so for man to be increased and multiplied, to fill the earth and to have dominion over it (Gen 1.28).

But there exists as well a second description of the creation of man, which the second chapter of the book of Genesis (vv. 4-25) preserves for us and which the philologists consider to be more ancient as a written formulation. There, the formation of man is not bound from the beginning with the differentiation of the sexes. God creates the first human, who has a masculine name, "Adam". But the name shows the quality of earthliness, not his sex. On this first and general human, God breathes his breath and establishes him as a "living soul". The differentiation of sex follows, only in order to serve the need for communion: "It is not good for man to be alone; let us make a helper for him who is like him" (2.18). And the distinction of the sexes is accomplished with the intervention of a special creative activity of God, a second formation: God imposes an "ecstasy" on Adam and takes one of his ribs and constructs the woman (2.21-22).

In this second description, the consciousness of sex is also the first expression of man's self-knowledge: Facing the existence which has come forth from his side, Adam gives himself a name, a name which arises from his relation to his partner. He is not longer simply "Adam", he becomes *ish* and she becomes *ishah* – he becomes a *man* since she is a *woman* (2.23). With the criteria of ecclesial hermeneutics, we must see in the image of the first and general human the undivided unity of human nature. But the natural similarity of flesh and bones (Gen 2.23) is not enough to ensure that unity of nature which would establish man as an image of the divine triadic unity. The triadic prototype of life is unity as a communion of love, a communion of separate and free hypostases, not a naturally given unity. So we return again to the necessity of the distinction of the sexes if the image or manifestation of the life of the uncreated is to be realized within the bounds of the created.

Facing the woman, Adam prophesies: "Because of this, man shall leave his father and mother and shall be joined to his wife and the two shall be as one flesh" (Gen 2.24). The communion of man and woman is intended to be an event of freedom which is completed in a natural unity. The naturally given bond with the parents is broken so that a new bond can be created of free choice and devotion, which results not only in living together, friendship, an ethical and spiritual relationship, but in a physical unity, which means a unity of life, literally a co-existence, an existence-with. This is the way in which the triadic prototype of life is realized within the limits of created nature.

Consequently, in the biblical perspective the distinction of the sexes, while it has its foundation in the nature of man – it is a manifestation or demonstration of his nature – does not have the needs and expediencies of nature in view, but that unity of nature which is a fruit of freedom from nature, a fruit of personal love. In other words, the distinction of the sexes does not function in man as it functions in the animals where it is exclusively subordinate to the natural necessity of propagation. In Adam's prophecy which interprets the reason or goal of the distinction of the sexes, the physical expediency of propagation does not appear at all – the natural unity "as one flesh" is determined as a unique goal, a unity which is the result of the free "joining" to the person of the other sex. But also in the description of the creation of man which the first chapter of Genesis (vv. 26-29) gives us, the perspective of increase and propagation of people appears as a result of a special *blessing* of God (v. 28), that is of a special gift which is offered to man, and not as a given physical necessity as in animals. Only *sin*, the failure of man to realize life in accordance with its triadic prototype, will upset this order and displace the object of the distinction of the sexes from being the "image" of God to the relentless necessity of physical perpetuation.

i. The power of love

The distinction of the sexes has its foundation in human nature, but it is not identical with this nature, just as it is not to be identified even with the hypostasis of man. It is one of the energies of the nature about which we have spoken above, one of the ways in which the existential reality of the nature operates, the unique, distinct and unrepeatable character of every specific human hypostasis. The science of psychology today assures us that the erotic urge does not appear in man simply at the age when it is needed to serve the propagation of the species. But from the first moment of his birth, the erotic impulse toward the mother constitutes the first possibility of a vital relationship – a possibility which makes up the personality itself of man and the beginning of his entry into the world of people, into the area of life as communion.

Without the distinction of the sexes and the erotic impulse which accompanies it, the fact of relationship, of communion, of love, of eros, would perhaps be defined at the level of behaviour, of communication, of a simple psychological bond. Thanks to the distinction of the sexes, eros is an impulse and presupposition of life, the fundamental presupposition for the realization and manifestation of the personal hypostasis of life. The personal hypostasis of man, even in its biological origin, is a fruit of the eros of two other people. But the composition itself and manifestation of the personhood of the subject is a result of the possibility of relationship, of communion, of erotic reference. The relationship of the infant with its mother is erotic, not of course because it intends the perpetuation of the species, but because it is a relationship constitutive of life. The mother transmits life to the baby, not metaphorically and symbolically, but literally and really: She gives it the nourishment which is a presupposition of life, and with it the caress, the affection, the first words which are addressed to it; that is, she gives it the first possibility of relationship, the feeling of a personal presence without which the baby can never enter the world of people, the world of language and of symbols, of existential identity and names.

The connection of sexual distinction with the creation of man "in the image of God" is not, then, by chance or simply metaphorical or by analogy. Man is the image of God since he is a person, a personal existence. But the person differs from the biological individual, precisely since his existence itself is not naturally given, but is realized as an event of erotic relationship and communion. The distinction of the sexes permits man to give a physical hypostasis (an hypostasis of nature) to his personal existence – permits the personal reference to be effected as an event constitutive of the hypostasis and unifying for the nature of man.

Therefore it is not chance either that God's relationship with man (the principal relationship constitutive of life as a personal hypostasis) is always portrayed by the erotic relationship of a man and woman. When Israel is unfaithful to God and worships idols, the prophets charge that he is committing adultery (Jer 13.27), dishonoring the uniqueness of the relationship by which God had elevated him to the place of the "beloved" (Hos 2.23; Rm 9.25). The relationship of God with his people, with each member of his people, is a nuptial secret, erotic, and this is the only reason, for the ecclesial interpretation at least, that a clearly erotic song, the Song of Songs, takes a place among the books of the Old Testament.

But the erotic relationship of God with Israel is only an image and copy of the union which God has realized with humanity in the Person of Christ and by means of his body which is the Church. This is the "great mystery" which the Apostle Paul describes in his Letter to the Ephesians (5.23-33) and which the parables of the Gospels portray with scenes taken from wedding dinners and banquets. In the New Testament, Christ is the bridegroom of the Church and the bridegroom of the soul of each one of us – God is passionately in love with the person of each human. And especially in the Gospel of John, eternal life which Christ comes to give us is defined by the verb "to know", which always renders the Hebrew word which means, in biblical language, the erotic relationship of a man and a woman: "Eternal life is this, to know you the only true God and Jesus Christ whom you have sent" (Jn 17.3).

In the patristic tradition, God himself in his internal triadic life will be defined as "the whole of eros", the fullness of continuous erotic unity: "This eros is love, and it is written, that God is love".[2] And this eros is *ecstatic*, "stimulating the erotic inclination of God" which founds and constitutes the

---

[2]Maximus Confessor, *Scholia on the "On the Divine Names" of Dionysius the Areopagite*, 4,17, *P.G.* 4, 268-269.

beings "outside him": "He, the cause of the universe . . .
through the superabundance of his erotic goodness . . . is
outside of himself . . . and it is as if he feels fascinated by . . .
love and eros; and he descends from the condition of pre-
eminence before the universe and of separation from the
universe."[3] The only way for man to describe the experience
of receiving this eros and his response to it is again the
relationship of man and woman: "Love for you has come
upon me as the love of women".[4] In the ascetical literature,
the copy of the love of God for man and of man for God
likewise is to be sought in the forms of human eros and
especially of bodily love, not of the idealistic forms of
platonic nostalgia: "Let bodily love be an example for you of
the desire for God".[5] "The most passionate lover of his own
beloved does not desire, as God desires the soul he desires to
repent.[6] "Blessed is the one who has acquired such desire for
God, as that which the passionate lover has for his beloved.[7]

If love as we usually know it expresses more a blind and
instinctive impulse for selfish pleasure and not the liberation of
the person from the necessities and demands of nature (given
that life is supposed to be accomplished as a loving co-
inherence of two persons), this is because we know love in its
fallen condition, we know it as *sin*, that is, as an existential
failure and loss of its purpose and goal. But even in the
condition of the fall and of sin, love makes possible the natural
union of two different hypostases and the formation of new
personal hypostases, because something is preserved from the
power to love which has been imprinted on our nature as an
image of God. It is the power of love which makes possible the
union not only of different hypostases, but also of different
natures, and shows man to be "a participant in the divine

---

[3]Pseudo-Dionysius the Areopagite, *On the Divine Names*, 4.13, *P.G.* 3,
712AB. cf. ET *The Divine Names and Mystical Theology* tr John D. Jones
(Marquette UP, Milwaukee, 1980) p. 145.
[4]Ibid. 709C. Page 144 in Jones' translation. cf. 2 Sam 1.26.
[5]John Climacus, *The Ladder of Divine Ascent*, Step 26 § 31. cf. ET by Colm
Luibheid and Norman Russell (Paulist Press, New York, 1982), p. 236.
[6]Nilus the Ascetic, *Epistles*, P.G. 79, 464.
[7]John Climacus, Step 30, § 5. cf. ET by Colm Luibheid and Norman Russell, p.
287.

nature", the whole man to be "co-inhering totally with the whole God and becoming all that God is, except for the identity of essence".[8] The writer of the Areopagitic texts sees an "obscure echo" of this power to love even in the dissolute who "desires the worst life in accord with an unreasonable lust".[9] And St Maximus Confessor recognizes even in the erotic attraction of animals without reason, as in the attractive power which forms the "common alleluia" of the whole creation, a single erotic impulse and movement turning back to the single form of divine life.[10]

All this means that for ecclesial anthropology, the distinction of the sexes neither serves simply the physical expedient of perpetuation of the species, nor only an extension of social rôles which permits the creation of the "cell" of social life which is the family. Before anything else, the distinction of the sexes in man and the erotic attraction of heterosexual existences leads the general erotic impulse placed in the nature to its "natural" end and purpose: it serves the imaging in nature of the triadic mode of life – the personal co-inherence of life within the limits of created nature. It intends finally the deifying union of man with God.

If man refuses this goal and purpose, love is perverted into an eneluctable *suffering* of the nature: The nature *suffers* love, endures it as a tormenting and always unfulfilled desire for existential completion and a relentless expedient for perpetuation of the species. Sin is precisely the failure of love to realize the goal which it has in view, which is the union of man with God. Love is transformed into an everlasting repetition of the tragedy of the Danaids, into an insatiable impulse for the satisfaction of nature, hedonism and pleasure of individual senses. It is no longer an event of communion and loving relationship, but a subordination of the other to subjective demand and the need for sensual pleasure.

[8]Maximus Confessor. *To Thalassios: On Various Questions relating to Holy Scripture*, P.G. 91, 1308AB. cf. *The Philokalia*, vol 2. tr G.E.H. Palmer, Philip Sherrard, Kallistos Ware (Faber and Faber, London, 1981), "Various Texts on Theology, the Divine Economy, and Virtue and Vice", 3.30, p. 216.
[9]*On the Divine Names*. IV, P.G. 3, 720BC. cf. Jones' translation p. 151.
[10]*Scholia on "On the Divine Names"*, P.G. 4, 268CD-269A.

Only when the love which is directed to the person of the other sex leads to the loving transcendence of physical individuality (which means: for man to go beyond his individuality, his private desires, needs and demands, to cease to aim at individual survival and to begin to live for joy of the other, from love for the other), only then is the way freed for man's response to the erotic call of God and for love to become a way of life and a gift of life. Therefore the love of Christ for the Church, to the point of the cross (Eph 5.23-33), is also an example of conjugal eros, the willing mortification of physical individuality if life is to be realized only as love and self-offering. First Christ incarnates the example of "real love" and makes possible our own erotic reference to his Person: "He first loved us," says Photius the Great, "while we were enemies and hostile. And he not only loved, but he was also dishonoured on our behalf and was smitten and crucified and counted among the dead; and through all these things he presented his love for us".[11]

Within the Church, which is the place of the Kingdom of God – the place where the triadic way of "real life" is realized – "there is neither male nor female" (Gal 3.28).

Within the Church we exist in the manner in which we will exist even after the death of our physical individuality: Not with the powers and abilities of our nature, its psychosomatic energies, but thanks to the love of God "who calls into existence the things that do not exist" (Rom 4.17) – thanks to his own erotic call which constitutes our existence as an event of communion with Him.

This does not mean that our nature is taken away within the space of the Kingdom. It means that the way by which our nature is hypostasized (becomes an hypostasis) is transformed. Nature does not become any longer an hypostasis (a particular living existence) thanks to its own functions and energies, but thanks to the call of God's love. Therefore we no longer have any need to pass by way of the natural possibility of the

---

[11]Photius, Patriarch of Constantinople, d. 895. The quotation is from the *Admonitory Enchiridion* of St Nikodemos of the Holy Mountain. p. 183, n. 1.

distinction of the sexes in order to realize our natural existence as an hypostasis of life, that is, of love and communion.

The gospel word wishes to mark this reality when it affirms that in the area of "real life" sexuality is abolished, the distinction of the sexes is abolished: "The sons of this age marry and are given in marriage; but those who are accounted worthy to attain to that age and to the resurrection from the dead neither marry nor are given in marriage; for they cannot die any more, because they are equal to angels and are sons of God, being sons of the resurrection" (Lk 20.34-36, *RSV*).

The resurrection which abolishes the marital relationship, as it also abolishes death, is a resurrection "from the dead". It presupposes the death of the autonomous physical mode for the composition of our hypostasis, the willing or unwilling death of the individual who draws his existence from the strengths and energies of his nature. It is necessary that a death interpose in order that "what is mortal may be swallowed up by life" (2 Cor 5.4, *RSV*). The *monastics* of the Church willingly brave this death. They refuse marriage, the natural way for the erotic self-transcendence of individuality and attempt the leap to hypostasize eros and the body in the mode of the Kingdom, to exist only by obedience and spiritual exercise, only by self-renunciation from nature, to draw existence and life only from the call of love which God addresses to man.

Accordingly, the monastics of the Church are the pioneers and the first-fruits of the Kingdom – the Kingdom which is being brought to birth secretly within the bosom of the Church. We others, the majority, have need of a "helper" (Gen 2.18) of the other sex in order to arrive, with the example of Christ's cross, at the death and resurrection which the monastics attain with a leap. And both roads – both the monastic and the married – are equally revered and considered worthy within the Church, since the goal of them both is the same: Life free from space, time, corruption and death.

j. The fall

The consciousness of a *fall* which has brought man down to a level of existence different from that for which he feels he was formed is not exclusively a part of the Judaeo-christian tradition. All peoples have this consciousness which is expressed in myths and symbols in almost every religion. This consciousness has inspired serious speculative turns in many philosophical systems.

But nevertheless for the Christian tradition the reference to the fall of man is not simply a particular twist to its anthropological theorizing, but the axis or "key" to understanding man, the world and history. On the one side the truth of the fall and on the other the truth of the *deification* of man define the fact of the Church itself and give meaning to its existence and its historical mission.

The Church's teaching on the theme of the fall is drawn chiefly from the interpretation of the texts of the Old Testament. The narrative of the creation of man in the first pages of the book of Genesis is completed by reference to the event of the fall, with an imagery astonishing in its wealth of meaning and with unrepeatable archetypical symbolism.

We read in the book of Genesis that God, when he had created man, planted a garden for his pleasure, a most beautiful garden in Eden, and settled him there. The image of the garden in all middle eastern religions functions as a symbol of ideal happiness – perhaps in contrast with the aridity and the bareness of the deserts which abound in these regions. Certainly, the drought of the desert is a symbol of death, while the rivers which irrigate the garden of Eden and the wealth of vegetation which adorn it give the picture of fullness of life.

Within this "garden of luxury", as the Scripture characterizes it, God places the first formed man "to work it and keep it" (Gen 2.15). Work in this first phase of human life is not "labour" – a slavery to the need for physical survival – but the organic continuation and extension of the creative work of God, the flowering of the creativity which characterizes man as an image of God, as a person.

At the same time, all the fruit of the plants in paradise are offered to man by God "for food" (Gen 1.29). Man's life of paradise does not represent a "spiritualized" condition or idealistic exaltation, as the moralists often imagine. Man's life, from the first moment, is realized by taking nourishment, the immediate use of the stuff of the world. Man lives and exists only in a direct and organic relationship with the world, with the stuff of the world. It is not an intellectual and theoretical relationship; man is not simply a spectator and observer or the interpreter of the world, but he is the one who employs the world directly as nourishment, takes it into himself and makes it his body. Only thus, only with this organic communion with the world is human life realized.

The extraordinary thing in man's state of paradise is that this taking of nourishment, which assures man his life, constitutes not only a practical relationship and communion with the world, but also a practical and vital relationship with God. God is the one who provides man his nourishment, the presupposition of life. He offers him every fruit and seed "as food". Every taking of food is a gift of God, a "blessing" of God, a realization of relationship with Him – a realization of life as relationship. Man's relationship with God in paradise is not an ethical or religious relationship, which means that it is not realized indirectly by the keeping of some law or by offering of prayers and sacrifices. It is man's life itself which is realized as a relationship and communion with God, the direct realization of life by the taking of nourishment, food and drink.

We find this same truth of the first pages of Genesis in the ecclesial action of the Eucharist, where the relationship of man with God – as it has been restored as a relationship of life "in the flesh" of Christ – is realized again universally within an event of eating and drinking: Man again takes his nourishment – the basic forms of nourishment which are bread and wine – as an event of communion of a now hypostatically divine-human communion: Body and Blood of Christ. The Holy Communion, the communion of man with God, is again a relationship of life by means of nourishment. Man does not draw his life from nourishment by itself, but from nourishment as a relationship and communion with God. He takes his nourishment as a gift of life which God offers to him; he draws life and existence from the event of communion with Him and not from the ability of his nature to survive fleetingly by means of nutrition. But this change of the mode of existence surpasses, however, the physical act of eating and drinking. Participation in the way of the Kingdom is not a passage to some "other" life, but making this life itself incorruptible, this life which is realized as a communion of nourishment. Therefore the image of the Kingdom of God in the New Testament is often a picture of a dinner where people "eat and drink at the table" which God has set for them (Lk 22.30).

God offered to the first formed people the possibility of life, of "real life", of incorruptibility and immortality, giving them the world, nourishment, as an event of communion with Him. But the realization of life as communion and relationship is nevertheless a fruit of freedom – there is no necessary or compulsory communion or relationship of love. This means that the life of paradise of those first-formed people included even the possibility of a different use of freedom: the possibility for human existence to be realized, not as an event of communion and relationship with God, but to be realized by itself alone, drawing existential strength from itself, from its created nature alone.

This possibility is expressively portrayed in the biblical narrative by using the symbol of the tree "of the knowledge of good and evil" (Gen 2.9,17). This too is a tree of paradise, but it is not included in the "blessing" which God offered to man – the eating of its fruit does not constitute fellowship and relationship with God. It represents precisely the possibility for man to take his nourishment – to realize his life – not as communion with God, but unrelated to and independent of God, to feed himself only for his own preservation, for the survival of his physical individuality, for man to exist not as a person, drawing an hypostasis of life from the communion of love, but to exist as a physical *individual*, as an existential unit which draws the survival of its hypostasis from its own powers, its created energies and functions.

God asks the first formed people not to eat of fruit from the tree "of the knowledge of good and evil". Can it be that he wishes to exclude them from the knowledge of ethical dilemmas, to keep them morally "unidimensional"? We must discern here that the terms "good" and "evil" do not have the conventional content of good and bad as we understand them today. They are not categories of conduct; they do not express the legal conception of socially useful and socially harmful. Here, as throughout the Holy Scripture, the terms "good" and "evil" show the possibility of life and the alienation from life which is the possibility of death. God makes this clear to these first formed people and warns them: "the day in which you eat from it, you will surely die" (Gen 2.17).

In these words of God, we do not have a threat of punishment, but a forecast and warning. If these first people eat from this tree, they do not simply make a mistake, they do not transgress some command which must be kept because it is given "from above". Eating the fruit of this tree will remove the presuppositions of life and lead them to death. They will have tried to realize life, not in the way which constitutes life (the triadic way of love and communion), but completely the opposite: by seeking to draw life from the created and therefore ephemeral capacities of their natural individuality, to exist as if each physical individual has its cause and its end in itself. "Good" and "evil" do not constitute here a simply conceptual antithesis – "evil" is not the open refutation of "good", but its counterfeit and perversion. There is a "good" and an "evil" way to realize life: this is the dilemma which is posed for the first formed people. The "evil" way advances the possibility of living from oneself, the possibility for the created thing to contain both its cause and its goal, to attain by itself, that is, equality with God and to divinize itself. But this is a lie, a false pursuit, which accepts as life the denial of life and leads undeterred to death. In the biblical picture, God wishes to dissuade man from precisely this knowledge of death – because death is a definitive knowledge and, once it is attained, it is too late to hold back its tragic consequences.

But the first people chose finally the way of "evil", the way of death. The warning which God directed to them underlines in the biblical narrative that their choice is made with full awareness of its consequences. However, there intervened a certain extenuating circumstance: In their decision they were influenced by the snake, the archetypical symbol of evil. In ecclesial hermeneutics, the snake here is an expression of the intervention of the *devil* or Satan, who constitutes a personal existence, spiritual, similar to the angels of God, the ministering spirits that God created before the world. The devil, though, is an existence in revolt, excluded from life, self-condemned to perpetuate the death which he first of all freely chose.

The snake directs his challenge firstly to the woman. And here the symbolism is not accidental. In the language of archetypes of life which the Scripture uses (the language of archetypical images which "signify" much more than concepts), the woman is the image of *nature*, in contradistinction to the man who is the symbol of the *essential principle (lógos)*. This contrast of nature and essential principle, feminine and masculine, does not represent an evaluative distinction, but portrays the experience which man has of the way in which physical life is realized: Nature has a "feminine" readiness to incarnate the event of life, but it needs the seed of the essential principle in order that this incarnation be realized. Without the pairing of masculine and feminine, life cannot exist. Without the intervention of the constitutive principle, nature is only a potential, not an existential event. And without its incarnation in nature, the existential principle is just an abstract concept, without substance.

And so the temptation to pervert the realization of life, precisely because it constitutes not only a theoretical challenge but a physical possibility, is accepted initially by the woman. The words which the snake addresses to her are frankly the "logical" imitation of the "good" – unfeignedly a principle which wants to deceive nature, to falsify the possibilities of life: "What is this that God has said to you? Not to eat from any tree of paradise?" The woman reacts, "We can eat from the fruit of the trees of paradise, but from the fruit of the tree that is in the middle of the garden God has said not to eat, lest we die." The snake does not persist in rough reproaches, he gives up immediately and takes another approach: "You will not die," he says, "because God knows that the day that you eat from this tree, your eyes will open and you will become like gods knowing good from evil." The biblical picture does not proceed further. The woman yields to this second temptation to equality with God and self-deification – nature agrees to attempt to have its life from itself. The first people taste the fruit of autonomy and existential self-sufficiency.

k. Consequences of the fall: nakedness

And so the fall of man is complete. We speak of a fall in order to show not a simply evaluative degradation, but a change in the mode of existence, a decline from life. The biblical narrative portrays this existential change, the consequences of the fall in unrepeatable symbols –

The sense of nakedness is the first consequence: "the eyes of the two of them were opened and they knew that they were naked and they sewed fig leaves and made aprons for themselves" (Gen 3.7). Until the time of the fall "the two were naked, both Adam and his wife, and they were not ashamed" (Gen 2.25). What, then, is the feeling of nakedness, the shame of nakedness which accompanies the fall? It is the awareness that the look of the other which falls on me is not the look of the beloved, of the one who loves me, whom I trust. It is the look of a stranger; he does not look at me with love, but sees me just as an object only of his desire and pleasure. The other's look objectifies me, transforms me into a neutral individual. I feel him taking away my subjectivity, my deepest and unique identity. To feel naked is the rupture of relationship, the revocation of love, the need to protect myself from the threat which the other now constitutes for me. And I defend myself with shame. I dress myself in order to save my subjectivity, to protect myself from the look of the other, not to be transformed into an object at the service of the other's individual pleasure and self-sufficiency.

Before the fall the body was wholly an expression and manifestation of personal uniqueness, a dynamic call for communion of life, for self-transcendence and self-offering through love. The feeling of nakedness and the shame for nakedness begin from the moment when life ceases to have love in view, and aims only for the self-sufficiency of the individual – for individual need, for individual pleasure. Therefore after the fall, nakedness ceases to be shame and is made a movement of ultimate trust and self-offering only in human eros. "In true eros, the soul veils the body," said Nietzsche, whose obstinate atheism did not always render useless the faculty within him to perceive the truth. And from the other side, a saint, Isaac the Syrian, completes his word: "Love does not know shame . . . Love is naturally unabashed and oblivious to her measure."[12]

The feeling of nakedness and the shame of nakedness are the clearest manifestation of the change which human nature undergoes in the fall: the image of God imprinted on the nature of man is made obscene and perverted (but without its being destroyed) – the image of God which is the personal mode of existence, the mode of the Trinity, of the love of persons, of the love which alone can unify the life and will and activity of nature. Personal freedom is subordinated (though never totally) to the individual need for physical self-exis-tence, is made an instinct, an impulse, a relentless passion. And so nature is fragmented, parcelled out in individuals who live each one for himself alone, individuals treacherous to each other and opposed to the claim of life.

1. Consequences of the fall: guilt

A second expressive image for the consequences of the fall in the biblical narrative is the appearance of guilt and the attempt at individual justification. The first people hear the steps of God who is walking in the garden in the early evening and fear overcomes them, so much fear that they hasten to hide "from the face of the Lord God" among the trees of the garden. Then God calls Adam, asks him why he is afraid, and Adam

---

[12] *The Ascetica Homilies of Saint Isaac the Syrian*, tr Holy Transfiguration Monastery (Holy Transfiguration Monastery, Boston, MA, 1984), Sermon 51, p. 245.

attributes the cause of fear to his nakedness. Even before God, Adam now feels naked; he even feels the look of God as stripping him, feels it as an attack on his individuality. God is no longer his intimate, his beloved. The relationship with Him is not a bond of love and a source of life. Even God is an "other", a second existence whose mere presence threatens to eliminate the autonomy of the individual.

"You have eaten, then, from the fruit of the tree of which I instructed you not to eat," says God. And Adam hastens to shift the responsibility: "The woman whom you gave me," he answers, "she offered me the fruit and I ate." And when God asks the woman, "why did you do it?" her own response is an evasion: "The snake deceived me and I ate" (Gen 3.8-13). The fall which has been accomplished, appears now with the individual's self-defence, the transfer of responsibility, the effort for individual justification.

If the feeling of nakedness and shame is a manifestation of the loss of the personal character of existence, the feeling of guilt, fear, the attempt to transfer responsibility and to justify oneself individually are manifestations of anxiety over the loss of life, of true life which does not die. It is anxiety in the face of death. We have not reached such a conclusion arbitrarily, but with the standards of the ecclesial method of interpretation of the biblical images. Let us ask ourselves particularly: What does Adam in fact fear when he hides from God? From what does he wish to protect himself when he transfers the responsibility to his wife? Perhaps he is afraid of some external threat? Perhaps he senses some objective danger? But, he has no previous experience of threat and danger. Normally he should be as fearless as the infant who stretches his hand out to grab the fire.

The easy answer of the moralists is usually that Adam is afraid because he has violated the command of God and now expects punishment. But the concept of transgression and of punishment is itself an image taken from subsequent experiences of the world after the fall. If we absolutize and see only a single interpretation of Adam's fear, we will leave gaps and create unanswerable questions: How is it possible for Adam to fear God whom he knows only as "a passionate lover" of man and a giver of life? If, even after the fall, the love of someone truly in love is ready to forgive and forget every fault of the beloved person, will the love of God fail to attain even these human standards? Is the love of God less than the human love of the true lover, of the affectionate father, of the patient mother? Does God not manage even what he asks from us, that we "forgive those who sin against us" as many times as they wrong us, "up to seventy seven times"?

But God is just, the moralists answer, and he must grant justice and punish transgression. But from what do they derive this "must" to which they subordinate even God? Does there exist, then, some necessity which limits the love of God, limits his freedom? If there is, then God is not God or at least he is not the God that the Church knows. A "just" God, a heavenly police constable who oversees the keeping of the laws of an obligatory – even for him – justice is just a figment of the imagination of fallen humanity, a projection of its need for a supernatural individual security within the reciprocal treachery of collective co-existence. Whatever tricks of sophistry the moralists may contrive in order to accommodate the love of God to justice, the edifices of their reasoning remain unsound. "As a grain of sand cannot counterbalance a great quantity of gold, so in comparison God's use of justice cannot counterbalance his mercy," says St Isaac the Syrian. The God of the biblical revelation and of ecclesial experience is not just: "Do not call God just, for his justice is not manifest in the things concerning you. . . . Where, then, is God's justice? . . . 'He is good,' (Christ) says, 'to the evil and to the impious.'"[13]

m. Consequences of the fall: the tragedy of creation

To this fundamental truth, which is the experience and certainty of the Church, many oppose a host of examples from the Scripture of punishments which God imposes or promises: The flood which drowned every living existence on the earth except for the ark of Noah; the fire and brimstone which destroyed Sodom and Gomorrah; the plagues of

[13]Ibid, Sermon 51, p. 244 and pp. 250–1.

Pharaoh; David who is punished for his sin by the death of Absolom; and in the New Testament the paramount image of the future judgement and retribution, the division of the just and unjust, the threat of hell where there will be "wailing and gnashing of teeth". To these biblical examples, people have added every evil in nature, seeing them as the "scourge of God", punishments revealing the wrath of God, earthquakes, floods, epidemics, etc.

But the Church separates the images of exemplary punishments from the truth which these images reveal. The fall of man is truth, and the fall does not have merely a legal content, but as we have tried to say here, it is a distortion of life in which the freedom of man brings down the whole creation – since human freedom is the unique possibility for every created thing to realize or not to realize the purpose of its existence. A distortion of life means an alienation and corruption of the laws or ways by which life functions. In all these biblical examples of man's punishment and in all the "divine scourges", the Church sees the consequences of the alienated function of the laws and ways of life, the consequences of the distancing of creation from "real life", the chasm which the rebellion of man has dug between the created and the uncreated. The paedagogical language of Scripture, especially of the Old Testament which is directed to a stubborn people, interprets these consequences by the principle image comprehensible to fallen humanity: the image of the wrathful God who punishes transgression.

But God is not vengeful; it is just that he respects absolutely the freedom of man and the consequences of this freedom. He does not intervene to remove the most bitter fruits of man's free choice, because then he would remove the truth itself of the human person and the astounding, in fact cosmic, dimensions of this truth. The love of God intervenes only to transform the free self-punishment of man into a salvific education. The culmination of this intervention is the incarnation of God himself, his acceptance in the divine-human flesh of Christ of all the consequences of man's rebellion "to death on a cross" and the transformation of these consequences into a relationship and communion with the Father, that is with eternal life.

Thereafter, without the consequences of the fall being eliminated in a way subversive to human freedom, the possibility present in paradise of a choice between life and death is restored to man again, the possibility of converting death into life after the pattern of the second Adam, of Christ, or of persisting in death, in hell which is "the evidence of not loving".

For the Church the fall of Adam, in its cosmic and age long dimensions which are shocking to the human mind, is a great tragedy revealing the infinite bounds of personal freedom, the universal dimensions of the truth of the person – finally, revealing the "glory" of God, the unceasing majesty of His image, which he has imprinted on human nature. This revelation the Church discerns within the tragedy of the fall, a revelation which gives meaning to the whole creation. "For the creation waits with eager longing for the revealing of the sons of God. ... We know that the whole creation has been groaning in travail until now" (Rom 8.19, 22 *RSV*). The universal adventure which begins in the garden of Eden is not a failure of God's work. This world of natural catastrophies, of wars, of plagues, of injustice, of crimes, the world full of the groaning of innocent victims, the cries of battered children, literally drunk with blood and tears, this world is nevertheless not a triumph of justice, but it is in the eyes of the faithful a triumph of freedom which wins inch by inch and step by step the journey to deification led by the hand by the love of God. "I consider that the sufferings of this present time are not worth comparing with the glory that is to be revealed among us ... because the creation itself will be set free from its bondage to decay and obtain the glorious liberty of the children of God" (Rom 8.18,21 *RSV*). A deification of man and of the world which would not be an event of freedom, this is what the failure of God's work would be. An unfree deification is something as contradictory as a concept of an unfree God, a paradox, life without reason or sense.

n. Consequences of the fall: anxiety before death

Let us return again now to the fear which made Adam hide from God after the fall. We can say that this fear is not the child of a legal guilt. It is not an expectation of punishment. It is the loss of that "openness to God" of which the Scripture speaks (1 Jn. 3.21), the rupture of the relationship with him, the awareness of responsibility for realizing life separated from God, the first experience of existential loneliness which is a first taste of mortality. Adam's fear is agony before death.

By very different roads, contemporary psychoanalytic experience is forming the view that the first experience of guilt and anxiety is born in man with the event of his birth, being cut off from the maternal body. If this view is confirmed, then it will not be very far from the biblical image of that first fear of Adam: The first feeling of "existing as an individual", even if unconscious, is also the first feeling of mortality, a first experience of a very profound loneliness, that is, the individual's inability to draw life from somewhere other than himself. Within man's nature itself it appears that there exists an instinctive distinction between the way of life and the way of death – a distinction between "real life", which is communicated and shared, and the mortal individualization of existence. If this is true, then the primitive fear of Adam is not only an image and symbol but an actuality which marks man in the depths of his soul from the first moment of his coming into the world.

The dialogue of God with the first people in Eden ends with the announcement and prophetic description by God of the remaining consequences of the fall. Let us enumerate them:

An unbridgeable hostility is fixed between the woman and the snake, between human nature and the devil. The hostility will reach a climax in the person of some descendant of the woman who will crush the serpent's head, the power of the devil, while the snake will hardly succeed in bruising his "heel". This descendant of Eve is, for the Church, Christ and this first prediction of his victory over the devil is the Scripture's proto-gospel, the first joyful message of man's salvation.

The sorrows and the groaning of woman are multiplied; she becomes a sensitive vessel and easily given to suffering. She does not cease to be the bearer of life, but life now is the perpetuation of nature, not of the person. The woman gives birth to her children, then, with much pain because each birth is also a further fragmentation of her body, a fragmentation of nature, an addition of autonomous mortal individuals. Her relationship with her husband, the eros which reveals the triadic Original of life, is transformed into a rupture with her husband – "Your desire shall be for your husband, and he shall rule over you" (Gen 3.16 *RSV*).

But the approach of the man to life, his relationship with the earth, with nature, with his nourishment and life will be a ground of pain and ceaseless affliction. The relationship of man with material nature of the world cannot be a personal relationship, a relationship with the principle of God's love which constitutes the world. The world becomes a neutral object which resists man's effort to subordinate it to the need and desire for his individual survival. The earth "brings forth thorns and thistles" and man earns his bread "by the sweat of his brow", until he himself returns to the impersonal neutrality of the objectified earth for his body to be dissolved in the ground, because "you are dust, and to the dust you shall return" (Gen 3.19 *RSV*).

o. Consequences of the fall: the "coats of skin"

The narrative of the fall of man in the Holy Scripture ends with his dismissal from the garden of pleasure, his exclusion from the "tree of life", from the possibility of immortality. This tragic result is crowned with an image which reveals the love of God, of the love which succeeds in eliminating the decisive character of the fall, to limit the evil which has been invoked, to relativize the irremediable. It is the image of the "coats of skin" which has especially drawn the attention of Christian interpreters: "And the Lord God made for Adam and for his wife garments of skins, and clothed them" (Gen 3.21).

For ecclesial hermeneutics, the coats of skins with which God clothes the first people, symbolize the biological hypostasis which seals the personal otherness of man. Before the fall, every energy of the biological-earthly nature of man exists (is realized and manifested) only as a revelation of the divine image: it constitutes personal otherness, life as loving communion and relationship. After the fall, the hypostasis of the human subject is biological, and the energies of nature (the psychosomatic energies) at the service of life as simply individual survival. Man does not cease to be a person, an image of God; it is only that this image is clothed now with the "coat of skin" of absurdity, corruption and mortality.

But this clothing with corruption and death proves to be a very great philanthropy of God and providence of His love. By dressing the human person with a biological hypostasis, God tolerates the consequence of the fall: The physical (psychosomatic) energies do not hypostasize the personal otherness of life as love, but the mortal individuality and its ephemeral life. By permitting even death as a consequence of this clothing, God limits man precisely to his biological individuality, placing a limit and end to sin, the failure of life and corruption, "lest evil become immortal".

And so death removes not man himself but the corruption which surround him. It does not touch the human person whom God called into being: it removes and abolishes the false hypostasis of life, the biological individuality which man has put on with the fall. Death, a result of sin, is turned against the phenomenological triumph of sin – autonomous biological individuality – and abolishes it. Death annuls the covering of corruption, freeing the existential possibilities of the human person.

The road, then, remains open after the fall for the person of man to become once more an hypostasis of life, no longer of a biological life, corruptible and temporary, but of an incorruptible and immortal life. This new existential possibility God inaugurates himself with his incarnation, becoming the beginning of salvation and renewal of the human race.

8

Jesus Christ

a. The scandal

The name "Jesus Christ" cuts the history of mankind in two, but at the same time it has constituted and still constitutes the greatest scandal for human thought. It is God who has become man, and such a union remains incomprehensible to logic and inaccessible in any way whatever to "positive" knowledge.

The Apostle Paul first noted that for the Greeks, at least, the concept of divine-humanity is really "foolishness" (1 Cor 1.23). The Greeks taught people correct reasoning and methodical knowledge, which cannot function without the definition of things. And things, whatever exists, are defined by their essence, that is, by a total of properties which make each thing that exists to be what it is. A flower is a flower since it has a stem and petals and sepals and stamens and a pistil; it cannot be a flower and simultaneously have feet or wings, eyes to see or a voice to speak. And so even God, in order to be God, must be infinite, unlimited, omniscient, omnipotent, life itself and principle of motion; he cannot be God and simultaneously have a material and limited body, need oxygen to breath and food for nourishment, become tired, be sleepy, be grieved, suffer bodily.

The opposition of Greek thought to the concept of divine-humanity was expressed powerfully within the bosom of the Christian Church itself. Two very characteristic expressions of this opposition were the heresies of *Nestorianism* and *Monophysitism* which troubled the Christian world for entire centuries and which never ceased to represent two tendencies or inclinations in the attitude of Christians.

Nestorianism[1] expresses our tendency to see in the person of Jesus Christ a human existence in his essence or nature, to see just simply a man, an individual instantiation of human nature, though endowed by God with special gifts and extraordinary abilities. This tendency survives very widely in that large number of people who speak with respect about Christ, but who recognize in his person merely a great moral teacher, a very important man who founded what is qualitatively the highest religion so far, or a social reformer who led humanity to important ethical accomplishments.

Correspondingly, Monophysitism[2] expresses our tendency to see in the person of Jesus Christ only an intervention of God in history, to see just simply the God who seemingly appears as a man, who is, that is, a "shadow" of a man and not man in his nature or essence. And this tendency survives in those people who want to maintain within Christianity a form of philosophical and ethical *dualism*, to maintain, that is, the unbridgeable polarization – which accommodates itself so well to human thought – between the divine and the human, the spiritual and the material, the eternal and the temporal, the sacred and the profane.

It is characteristic that from his view-point, the psychiatrist Igor Caruso (to whom we referred in the previous chapter) sees revealed in these two heresies two more general tendencies or propensities of human psychology. Each of these, if it is absolutized, leads to that heretical image of life which we call neurosis. Caruso recognizes the historical offspring of such neurotic tendencies in many expressions of an absolutized anthropocentrism or an equally absolutized idealistic interpretation of life and of truth. In fact, we can discern a clear Nestorianism in the optimism of rationalism, in the "efficiency" of moralism, in the overvaluation of historical criticism, in the mythologizing of human science, in the

[1]Founded by Nestorius, Patriarch of Constantinople (380-451).
[2]Founded by Eutyches, a priest in Constantinople (378-454).

scientific demythologizing of metaphysics, in the absolutization of politics and organization, in the priority of economic
and productive relationships. And we can see the monophysite
reaction expressed in puritan idealism, in contempt for the
physical man, in distrust for the body and its functions, in the
fear of eros and sexual life, in the "de-spiritualization" of
structures, in the mythologization of visible authority, in the
mysticism of infallible leadership.

Given, then, these antithetical tendencies of human psychology, the language of the Church seeks to fix the boundaries of
the truth of her experience of God's incarnation, His incarnation in the historical person of Jesus Christ. In the Third,
Fourth, Sixth and Seventh Ecumenical Councils, over four
full centuries, the Church struggled to save the truth of the
incarnation of God from its falsification by an intellectual
schema and axiomatic "principle". The "Christ" of the
heresies was an ethical example of a perfect man or an abstract
idea of a fleshless God. In neither case is the life of men
changed in any essential respect, the living body of man
remains condemned to dissolve in the ground and the individual or collective "improvements" of human life are a farce, an
absurdity, or bare deception.

The Church did not struggle for four full centuries over an
abstract metaphysic or to safeguard an ethical example. She
did not even struggle for the "soul" of man; she wrestled to
save his body. Can the body of man, the flesh and not only the
soul, be united with God "without confusion, without
change, without division, and without separation"?[3] Can
human nature constitute a single event of life together with the
divine nature? If yes, then death does not exist. Then, the body
is sown in the ground like wheat in order to bear fruit a
hundred times over and man can realize the fullness of life.

She wrestled for four centuries to save the body of man
from the absurdity of death, and to declare that the humble
stuff of the world, the flesh of the earth and of man, has the
possibility of being united with the divine life and the

[3]From the Chalcedonian Definition, the statement of the Fourth Ecumenical
Council in 451 A.D. held in the city of Chalcedon. – tr.

corruptible to be clothed in incorruptibility. It was a struggle
and a contest so that our conventional everyday language
would be able to signify the dynamics of life revealed by the
flesh of the Word. Along with language there are the exercise
of the artist to speak the same truth with a brush, not
figuratively or symbolically, but impressing on the drawing
and in the colour the rendering incorruptible and the glory of
human flesh; and the artistic song of the architect who
"rationalizes" stone and clay and in whose building what
cannot be contained is contained, the fleshless is made flesh,
and the whole creation and the beauty of creation is justified;
and the hymn of the poet and the melody of the composer, an
art which subordinates the feelings instead of being subordinated to them, revealing in this submission the secret of life
which conquers death.

b. Self-emptying

To the opposition of the Greeks to the possibility of two
different natures or essences being united in one single
existence, the theology of the Fathers and of the Ecumenical
Council answers: this possibility exists in regard to God and
man since both divinity and the humanity have a common
mode of existence, the person. We have seen in the preceding
that personal otherness and freedom from every natural
predetermination, in accordance with the experience of the
Church, is God's mode of existence: the Person precedes the
Essence; it hypostasizes the Essence; it makes it to be an
hypostasis, a concrete existence. And the image of this divine
mode of existence has been imprinted on human nature. Even
if it is created and given, even human nature exists only as a
personal otherness and a potential for freedom from its
createdness – from every natural predetermination. Man was
formed not only "in the image", but also "in the likeness" of
God (Gen 1.26): His personal existence constitutes the possibility of man's attaining at some time the freedom of life
which characterizes God himself, that is, eternal life which is
not bound by natural limitations. The first Adam refused to
realize this potential. God, then, intervened, not in order to

compel man to be like Him, but in order to be himself like man, by guiding the personal potential of human nature to the extreme accomplishment of hypostatic union with Divinity – an accomplishment unattainable even for man before the fall.

But God did not unite himself with man straight away in that situation where the potential ending of the journey toward his likeness with God could guide Adam. The historical person of Jesus Christ is a human particular like all the particulars after the fall – a separate particular, limited and conformed in everything to the measure of the createdness of human nature and the limitations of nature. Only in some very few moments, on Mt Tabor, did Christ reveal the real consequence of the union of God with man – the transfiguration of man into "glory", a manifestation of God. In all the rest of Christ's life on earth, the existential manifestation of the life of God is "in restraint". The Church speaks of an "emptying" of God in the person of Christ, of a willing "voiding" or renunciation of every element directly revelatory of his divinity: "he emptied himself, taking the form of a servant, becoming conformed in the body to our humility" (Phil 2.7; 3.21).

This "emptying" of divinity in the person of Christ is a fruit of divine personal freedom, of the freedom of the incarnate Son and Word of God. It does not alter, nor does it affect the real union of the divine and human natures of Christ. Free from every predetermination of Essence or Nature, God can hypostasize in his Person not only his own Being (his Essence or Nature), but also the being of man. And by hypostasizing simultaneously the two natures in one personal hypostasis, he preserves the natural properties of each one, without being subjected to any necessity for the existential realization of these properties: Therefore he can "suppress" or "empty" the "glory" of his Divinity, as he can raise the weight of his material humanity when he walks on the waters of the lake. If the Person alone is that which hypostasizes Being, then no necessity of nature (divine or human) precedes in order to limit the existential manifestation of personal freedom.

c. "Without confusion" and "without division"

God assumes human nature and makes it a participant in his own divine Nature by hypostasizing the common personal mode of existence of the two natures in a single existence, in one person. This one person is the incarnate Word, the second Person of the Holy Trinity "in flesh", the only Son of the Father "become flesh". He is Jesus, the Christ of God.

The union of the two natures in Christ is *without confusion* and *without division*. The two natures are not confused; the difference between the two natures is not eliminated. The Divinity and the humanity each retain their own properties in one undivided existential realization, in the one person of Christ. The Church confesses Christ as perfect God and perfect man – there is no distortion or diminution or falsification either of his human or of his divine being.

But all these formulas are in danger of being understood as abstract concepts, if we ignore the mode by which the person hypostasizes nature (causes it to be a real existence) and, consequently, the union of natures. We must not forget that nature exists only as a personal hypostasis, only "in persons". And the person hypostasizes nature, since it summarizes in a single existential event, in the event of its own otherness and freedom, all the energies of its nature: volitional, rational, creative, loving and every other energy. We know nature only as an event which has been given effect, only by means of its energies which are carried and expressed existentially by the person. Nature without energies is only an abstract concept, an insubstantial intelligible "being". Like the person without a nature (whose energies it hypostasizes existentially), it is merely an abstract "principle".

The danger that we might understand the union of the two natures in Christ as an abstract theoretical "principle" by reference to "beings" which are simply intelligible and unrelated to any existential realization has been noted by the Church in the case of the heresies known as *Monotheletism* and *Monenergism*.[4] This heresy accepts that Christ has two natures, divine and human, but maintains that the union of the two

---

[4] Sergius, Patriarch of Constantinople (610-638), was the chief representative.

natures results in one personal will and energy of the incarnate God the Word.

But only one will means only one nature, because a second nature which is not given effect as an existential event is in fact non-existent. If Christ had only a divine will and energy, then his human nature is in fact insubstantial; he was himself an existentially inexplicable semblance of man and humanity remained unassumed by the Divinity and unhealed.

For the Church Christ is the person of the incarnate God the Word, a person who hypostasizes in a particular existential event both the divine and the human natures. The particular existential event is his personal otherness and freedom which summarizes and manifests the energies of the two natures. The person has priority over the nature (it gives existence and hypostasis to the nature). Personal difference and freedom summarize and manifest the natural energies without being subordinated to them. Thus, Christ's personal freedom is not subordinated to the energies of the two natures, but subordinates them and therefore orders them and reveals "his human will following and not resisting or opposing, but rather submitting to his divine and all-powerful will".[5]

Consequently, the precedence of the divine will in Christ is not a natural necessity; it is not that the divine will is imposed on the human by the force of its natural omnipotence. But this precedence is an accomplishment of Christ's personal freedom and, therefore, the Church proposes it in opposition to the use of freedom which the first Adam made. The first Adam refused to realize life (the personal existence of his nature) in the way of life, as a communion of love and erotic self-transcendence. His personal freedom (a manifestation and management of the natural energies which make up the event of existence) turned the volitional energy of his nature from the way of life to the way of death: he distorted life into individual survival, into an autonomous natural self-existence. And nature, existentially autonomous, is given effect as a necessity of life for its own sake, as an instinctive will for survival, for dominance, for perpetuation. Nature is made

---

[5] St Gregory Nazianzen, *Theological Orations*, IV, § 12.

autonomous by the personal possibility of life. The natural energies are untied from the freedom of the person (their personal management and expression); they become an existential purpose in themselves, a relentless necessity. Personal existence is given effect subordinate to nature and so to its createdness and, therefore, it results in death – the last natural necessity of the created.

In contrast, the second Adam, Christ, by his personal freedom subordinates the will of his human nature to the will of his divine nature, to the will of real life which is effected as a communion of obedience to the Father, as a self-surrender to His love. The will of Christ's divine nature is the common will of the Persons of the Holy Trinity, the will of life, the freedom of love – a freedom from every necessity and, therefore, synonymous with eternal life. To this will of freedom which realizes life as self-transcendence and subordination of love, Christ subordinates his natural human will, and with this subordination he brings about healing, the cure of human nature. Human nature is no longer an autonomous necessity of self-preservation; it is not the attempt at self-existence by what has been created ending inescapably in death. Now there exists a Person who sums up the energies of human nature in the free realization of life; now human nature shares by means of the will of the Son in the life of the Trinity. Its created character, its materiality, does not impede its hypostatic and existential union with Divinity, since what makes up existence is not the nature in itself and its energies (materiality or spirituality or immateriality), but the person who hypostasizes it.

d. Perfect God and perfect man

It is astonishing the attention the Church paid to the attempt to mark with exactness of expression the limits of the event which was completed in Christ, so that the union of God with man not be exhausted by that expression nor be supported by categories from conventional logic. Rather, she wished that the formulation of this truth be safeguarded from every misinterpretation which would alter man's capacity to share in the immortalization of what is mortal being completed in the incarnation of the Word.

We speak, then, in principle of the incarnation of God in the person of Christ, of God's becoming man. "We say that God has become man, not that man has become God."[6] When we refer to Christ, we do not define someone who is essentially a man to whom the Divinity has been united; there is no pre-existent human hypostasis to which God the Word has been added. But God the Word "has framed" for himself living flesh "from the pure blood of the virgin", being himself the hypostasis which is made incarnate by this extraordinary conception. The assumption of human nature by the Word followed the way in which nature as an existential event is given effect: It has as a beginning the womb of a woman. There is formed and grows the living flesh which reveals the hypostasis or the person.

We speak of the incarnation of the Son and Word of God, of the second Person of the Holy Trinity. This does not mean that the Word acts independently of the other Persons and alone effects the assumption of humanity. The Church recognizes in the event of the incarnation of God the Word a common activity of the Persons of the Holy Trinity. Not that either the Father or the Spirit are in any way made incarnate with the Word. But while the distinction of the divine Hypostases is not removed and only the Hypostasis of the Word assumes human flesh, still the will and activity of the Trinity remains common to them even with respect to the incarnation – the uniqueness of God is preserved, the unity of divine life. This single totality of life and will and activity of the Divinity is summed up by Christ in his divine-human hypostasis: "for in him the whole fullness of deity dwells bodily" (Col 2.9 *RSV*).

We confess Christ to be perfect God, but also perfect man. The whole Divinity is united in his person with the whole humanity. Every property and every energy of the entire human nature has been assumed by Christ, nothing human has remained outside of this assumption. The initiative for the

[6] St John of Damascus, *On the Orthodox Faith*, III, 47.

assumption is, however, in the one who assumes, who acts
singly in respect of his hypostasis and *triadicly* in respect of will
and grace. But what is assumed is not a passive factor in the
assumption. God in becoming incarnate does not compel
human nature, he does not use nature as a neutral material for
realizing his will. Human nature is offered to be assumed by
God by a free personal consent – the nature is offered *entirely*
and its self-offering is effected *uniquely* (since nature exists and
is expressed only personally): it is the consent of the Virgin
Mary, the free acceptance on her part of the will of God,
which makes possible the meeting of the divine will with the
human in the event of the incarnation of the Son and Word.
"Behold, I am the handmaid of the Lord; let it be to me
according to your word" (Lk 1.38 *RSV*).

In these words is expressed a stance of self-surrender and
self-offering, of acceptance of the will of God, and of
absolute trust in his love. No claim to autonomy, no demand
for self-protection. Mary offers herself for this conception
and pregnancy only out of obedience to God; she disposes her
existence in order that his will be done. And so the conception
which is accomplished is free from any natural intentionality,
free from every necessity and bondage to desire, lust,
pleasure, from every instinct of reproduction and perpetuation. The natural energy of motherhood is transformed from
an independent biological function into a personal event of
free consent, of obedience to God, abandonment to his
providence. And it is precisely freedom from natural necessity
which shows Mary "even after giving birth to be Virgin".

We say in the language of the Church that the union of God
with man, the incarnation of God the Word is an event
"transcending nature". This means in principle: an event of
reciprocal freedom (of God and of man) from every natural
predetermination. In the person of the Blessed Virgin and
Mother of God "the limits of nature have been defeated", the
presuppositions and necessities which dominate the created in
its autonomy are removed by the uncreated. But the Uncreated, in his incarnation from the Virgin, also transcends the
mode of the uncreated and begins to exist in the mode of the
created; he who is outside of time enters time and he who is

uncontainable is contained and he who is before all ages is an infant and the impalpable assumes the dimension of individuality. For humanity to transcend nature is to be released from the limitations of createdness and the necessities of fallen autonomy. And for Divinity to transcend nature is freedom even from the freedom of unlimited transcendence of every predetermination or need – the event that transcends nature is that God "has come up to nature, that is, he has arrived at that which is less worthy and which he did not possess".[7] From this double transcendence the only absolute existential event for the Church is revealed and that is the Person of God and his image imprinted on the personal existence of man.

e. Theotokos

The Church recognizes in the person of the Blessed Theotokos that creature who – alone within all God's creation, material and spiritual – attained to the fullness of purpose for which the creation exists, to the fullest possible unity with God, to the fullest realization of the possibilities of life. Her consent to the incarnation of the Son was not only a harmonizing of the human will with the will of God, but a unique existential event of co-inherence of the life of the created and the life of the uncreated: our Lady was counted worthy to share by her natural energy (the energy of will, but also of motherhood) in the common activity of the Divinity, that is in the very life of God. Her physical life, her blood, the biological functioning of her body, was identified with the life given effect in the incarnate hypostasis of God the Word. God the Word lived hypostatically as a part of her body; God lived within her womb with her own flesh and blood; her own natural created energy was identified with the energy of the life of the uncreated.

The Theotokos did not simply "lend" her biological functions to God the Word, because a mother does not "lend" her body to her child, but she builds up his existence with her flesh and her blood just as she forms the "soul" of her child with her

[7]Maximus Confessor, *Scholia on the Divine Names*, P.G. 4, 229C.

nursing, speech, caressing, affection. The Church insists that
the Son and Word of God did not simply assume flesh in his
incarnation, but a "flesh animated by a reasonable and spiritual
soul",[8] just as is the flesh of every human fetus. Christ
assumed human nature with the whole of the energies of body
and soul which go to make it up and express it. And the symbol
of the Theotokos does not stop at constructing the flesh of
Christ, but extends even to what we could call formation of
his soul, of his human psychology, since the mother is the
source and ground for the articulation of the first mental
experiences, of the first awareness, of the first baby-talk, of
the progressive entry of the child into the world of names and
symbols, the world of people.

To be Mother of God, then, the Virgin Mary identified in
her existence the life of the created with the life of the
uncreated; she united in her own life the creation with its
creator. And so every creature, the entire creation of God,
finds in her person the gate of "true life", the entrance to the
fullness of the existential possibilities. "In her all creation
rejoices, the company of angels and the race of men". In the
language of the Church's poetry, every image which includes
nature is ascribed to our Lady, in order to exhibit exactly the
entire renewal of the created which was accomplished in her
person. She is "heaven" and "fertile earth" and "unhewn
mountain" and "rock giving drink to those who thirst for life"
and "flourishing womb" and "field bringing forth atone-
ment". And the inimitable "semantics" of orthodox iconography translates the figurative statement of these images at one
time in outline and at another in colour. It represents the
Theotokos and throne of divinity, either as holding a child or
praying, or sweetly kissing the Child, or "reclining" at the
Nativity of Christ or at her own falling asleep. She is the new
Eve who recapitulates nature, not in that autonomy contrary to
nature and in death, but in that participation in the Divinity
which transcends nature and in the realization of eternal life.
Because her own will restores the existential "end" and
purpose of creation generally, she gives meaning and hope to

[8]St John of Damascus, *On the Orthodox Faith* III, 46.

the "eager longing of creation". When the faithful seek the intercession of the Theotokos for their salvation, they are not seeking some kind of juridical mediation, but that their own ineffective will be contained within her own lifegiving will, her will which affirms the saving love of the incarnate God.

f. Historical co-ordinates

In assuming human nature, God intervenes in time and places himself in human history. Jesus Christ is an historical person: He is born in a specific time and place, from a mother whose genealogical tree is rooted in and branches from a specific tribe of Israel, the royal family of David. And so he himself is a Hebrew by race, placed in the social conventions of the hellenized world of the Roman empire, subordinate to the ruling political structures in the land of the Hebrews occupied by the Romans.

His own name is a composite of the two languages and traditions which form the historical co-ordinates of his time period and will form the historical flesh of the first Church: *Jesus* is a Hebrew name, *Christ* is a Greek word. With "Jesus" we hellenize the Hebrew "Jeshua", derived from a verbal root which means "I save", "I help". And the word "Christ" is an adjective used as a noun derived from the Greek verb for "I anoint" and means the "one who has been anointed", he who has received "anointing". In the Hebrew tradition, anointing with oil or myrrh was the visible sign of elevation to the rank of king or priest, a sign that the one anointed was chosen by God to serve the unity of the people or the relationship of the people with the Lord of Hosts. But the special Christ of God was, within the Scriptures, the expected Messiah and therefore the word "Christ" had become identified conceptually with the word "Messiah". Combining the proper name "Jesus" with the title of rank "Christ", the Church indicated the historical person and interpreted the fact which he incarnated.

Luke the Evangelist gives us the chronological reference points for the appearance of John the Baptist's preaching and consequently of the beginning of Christ's public life. He specifies the year which the Roman emperor is completing on the throne: "in the fifteenth year of the rule of Tiberius Caesar". This historical "mark" would be enough for a very exact chronological determination. But Luke persists with the scholasticism of an expert historian and so provides possible controversies about the historicity of Jesus. He states the chronology with reference to the local governors: "Pontius Pilate being governor of Judaea, Herod being tetrarch of Galilee, Philip his brother tetrarch of Iturea and Trachonitis, and Lysanius being tetrarch of Abilene". The political rulers are not enough, but he adds as well the chronological definition afforded by the terms of office of the religious rulers of Israel: "while Annas and Caiaphas were high priests" (Lk 3.1-2).

Luke's sensitivity to exact chronology would be justified many centuries later when the wave of atheism in Europe after the "Renaissance" tried to prove the person of Christ to be mythical and unsubstantial, thereby giving an easy solution to the evaluation of his divine-human hypostasis against the "foolishness" and "scandal". Successive generations of investigators in the last centuries have engaged in an extensive and many sided inquiry into the historical credibility of the Gospels: chronologies, references to persons, officials of the period, places, occurrence of events, came under the scrutiny of philology and historical criticism of the texts. Their verification was sought in the discoveries of the archeological spade. Christian apologetics cited a series of extra-Christian references to the person of Christ which appeared to confirm his intervention in history: Pliny the Younger (c. 112 A.D.), Tacitus (c. 115), Suetonius (c. 120), but also earlier references like the famous *testimonium* of Flavius Josephus (c. 93), the chronicle of the Samaritan, Thallus, written in Rome (a little before or a little after 60), the letter of the Syrian Mara Bar Sarapion (73 A.D.). By various routes, scientific investigation has verified the historicity of the person of Jesus Christ – without interpreting the fact which this Person made incarnate.

In the second "line of defence", western rationalism of the last centuries has invoked the "mythologizing" of the historical person of Christ by the first Christian community. The "logic" of this interpretation was not trivial. We draw almost the whole of our information about the historical person of Jesus Christ from the texts which the first Christian community wrote for itself – Gospels, Acts, letters of the Apostles. But this information expresses exclusively the idealized proclamation of the person of Christ, his identification with the messianic expectations, the religious pursuits, the missionary intentions of the first Christian community. There must exist, consequently, a difference and distance between the "historical Jesus" and the "Christ of the apostolic proclamation" which the Gospels preserve. In order for us to transcend this distance and to re-establish the historical truth about the person of Jesus, we must cleanse the gospel texts of the probable elements of "idealization" and keep only that information which can be proved historically indisputable. Of course, the problem which arises is: With what criteria will the "cleansing" of the gospel texts be undertaken and how far will it extend? To confront this question in practice has resulted in the creation of a variety of schools, tendencies and methods of interpretation, especially in the Protestant world, where each one confronts a different range of questions about the gospel narrative, arriving sometimes at the entire denial of the "supernatural" element, of the miracles and of the Resurrection of Christ.

All this speculation is, however, a consequence of a particular understanding of knowledge which especially characterizes western European man and, by extension, the type of man which the western way of life forms. We have spoken in earlier pages about this demand for "positive" knowledge, the search for certainties which every human understanding can possess with assurance, without the uncertainty of controversies. It assumes an individualistic attitude to life, an attitude of individual security, assured self-sufficiency, a culture of the "rights of the individual" – that is, a way of life at the extreme opposite of the ecclesial mode of existence. Of course, in preceding pages again, we have noted that the conclusions of the "positive" sciences as they are called (both physics and historical and anthropological investigations) tend today to a theory of knowledge which proves that "positive", objective and definite knowledge is unattainable. But it is difficult to restrain by theoretical efforts western man's demand to master knowledge individually and to exhaust it within the limits of his subjective capacities for knowledge. It is difficult because this demand constitutes a fruit of a general attitude and way of life. In contrast to the ecclesial realization of life (life as a dynamic achievement of loving self-transcendence and loving communion) it is literally an heretical understanding of what it is to live and to be true.

However, within these same limits of western theology, many interpreters have proved the historical value of the gospel narratives and the groundlessness of the separation of the "historical Jesus" from the "Christ of the apostolic preaching" with thoroughness as well as with rational arguments. For someone of the western type and attitude, this apologetic assurance of the value of the Gospels has, without anything else, a pedagogical usefulness and can strengthen "weak consciences". But the strengthening of "weak consciences" by apologetics has a clear and very definite limit: it can prove that the Gospels do not narrate myths, but real events certified by evidence verified many times over. Apologetics cannot, though, interpret the events of the gospel narratives, to bring to light the causes and the purpose of these incidents. No apologetic can certify the divine-humanity of Christ, the victory over death and the renewal of the created which was realized in the historic person of Jesus. And without the foundation of the truth of the incarnation of God and the deification of man, the gospel teaching stays an admirable, but finally utilitarian moralization, and the references to the miracles of Christ represent only an essentially uninterpreted supernatural "paradox".

g. "Source" and "sources"

In radically disputing the objectified "authority" of the Papacy, Protestantism proposed the Bible as the exclusive *source* of Christian truth. The Bible contains the complete truth of the revelation of God in an objective and definitive way. It is a text which makes the word of God directly accessible to us as an objective given without our needing supplements to revelation or intermediaries for faith and the reception of the divine word.

The Roman Catholic "counter-Reformation" objected to this absolutization of the authority of the Bible by Protestantism, proposing that there are two *sources* of Christian truth: the Holy Scripture and the Sacred Tradition. The "College of Bishops" expresses and administers the Sacred Tradition, but only by means of its "infallible" head, the Pope of Rome, who is defined as the "visible head of the whole Church" (*visibile caput totius Ecclesiae*). By his sanction, the ecclesial Tradition acquires genuine authority. All those ways by which the revelation of God is formulated and interpreted constitute this Tradition: Ecumenical Councils, opinions of the Fathers, liturgical practice, creeds, rules of life.

Whether the Scripture alone or the Scripture together with the Tradition, it is still a matter of the source or the sources by which the individual derives the truth "from the object"; it is a matter, that is, of the need for objective authority, the need of western man to be assured individually that he possesses an indisputable truth – even if this assurance is achieved by his submission to an idolized schematization of the "infallible", to the authority of supernatural revelation, or to the authority of science, to the divine inspiration of the texts of Scripture or, later, of the texts of Marx or any other ideology, to the "infallibility" of the Vatican or to the "infallibility" of Moscow or any other "see". The history of western man is a dialectic of submission and rebellion, where rebellion means in each case the choice of a different authority, consequently of a new submission, while the goal remains always the same – individual security, the protection of individual certainty about the truth to be believed.

Aside from the blood which was spilled (by the "holy wars", the "Holy Inquisition", the tortures which were established as an "investigative method in the trials of heretics"), enough ink was spilled to defend the authority of the Vatican, the "infallibility" of the Pope. Blatant forgeries of history were enlisted: that Peter was the first Bishop of Rome, that he exercised a primacy of power over the other

Apostles and subsequently bestowed this power to his successor Bishops of Rome, that Constantine the Great assigned the government of the western Roman state to the Pope with imperial rights ("pseudo-Donation of Constantine"), that very ancient canons treated the Pope as the supreme head of ecclesiastical – and also of political – power ("pseudo-Isidorean Decretals"), that Cyprian already in the 3rd century preached the papal primacy ("pseudo-Cyprian writings") and many others. But ample ink has been spent as well by Protestants to defend the inspiration of Scripture, the immediate revelation of God within the biblical text alone. It has been maintained that the writers of the Bible were simply passive instruments without their affecting the writing, even by influencing the style or punctuation of the texts; they merely lent their hand writing mechanically what the Holy Spirit dictated to them. And this because only such a rational inspiration could assure supernaturally and without contradiction the infallible authority of the texts and give to the faithful the certainty that the Bible could possess the truth.

Within such a climate, scientific dispute about the historical credibility of the Scriptures or the supports for the Tradition took away the foundation of "faith", that is, of submission to authority. Western man had to choose between atheism and the emasculation of his reason, or to accept compromise with a censored version of the gospel narrative, stripped of every "supernatural" element, suitable only for morally uplifting use, or even for political exploitation.

The life and practice of the undivided Church, like its historical extension in the theology and spirituality of the Orthodox Churches, knew neither one nor two sources of infallible authority. This does not mean that it disregarded or underestimated the meaning and the authority of the Holy Scripture and the Sacred Tradition. But it refused to separate truth from the realization and experience of the truth, the realization of life "in truth". Before any formulation, the truth is an *event*: the historical realization of the triadic mode of "real life". It is the body of Christ, the Church. The event of life which is the Church precedes both Scripture and Tradition – as his divine-human hypostasis precedes the teaching of

Christ, and without this hypostasis of life the gospel word remains, perhaps, a wonderful teaching, but unable to save the human race from death.

Scripture and Tradition define the truth and revelation of God to people without exhausting them. The words "truth" and "revelation" do not mean for the Church some "supplement" to our knowledge unattainable by our scientific or other reasonable method; they are not some "articles of faith" which we must accept without contradiction because they have been given to us in a "supernatural" way, such that no one would dare to dispute them. For the Church, truth and revelation refer to God who reveals himself to people as "real life". And life cannot be revealed with concepts "about" life, but only as an existential realization accessible to man. God's mode of being incarnate in an historical person – in the Person of Christ who realizes life free from death – is the truth and revelation of life. Christ is "the way and the truth and the life" (Jn 14.6) and remains "yesterday and today the same" (Heb 13.8) as the way and mode of existence of his body, the Church.

We know, consequently, the truth and revelation not simply by reading the Holy Scripture and the "credal" texts of the Tradition, but we verify these texts with our participation in the Church's mode of existence, in the way of the triadic prototype of life. We transform our individual approach to the texts into an ecclesial communion of the truth which the texts mark out. Outside of this communion, the ecclesial mode of existence, there exists neither truth nor revelation, but only some religious knowledge better or worse than other analogous knowledge. In order for us to know the word of the Holy Scripture, we must study it incarnate in the ecclesial Body of Christ, in the persons of the saints, of our spiritual fathers who "give us birth" into the life of the ecclesial communion.

The reading of the Holy Scripture in the undivided Church and afterwards in the Orthodox Church constitutes an act of worship: that is, an act of communion of the ecclesial Body. We communicate with the word of the Apostles who became "witnesses" and "observers" of the "manifestation" of God (they heard and saw and handled his historical revelation), we

communicate with them by reading their texts, not as historical information, but accepting their testimony as a confirmation of life and unity of the eucharistic body. Every
eucharistic gathering is also a revelation in practice of the
gospel word; it is the realization of the life of people, living
and dead, according to the model of the triadic unity, beyond
corruption and death. This is the Gospel, which we celebrate
every time in the Eucharist by accepting the reading of the
word of the Apostles as confirmation of our direct experience
there.

The gospel word of the Apostles is a word and revelation of
Christ, not because Christ dictated it to them by some form of
mechanical "inspiration", but because the Apostles wrote
down the relationship of life which they realized with Him,
the same relationship of life which constitutes the eucharistic
body in unity. They wrote down the word and revelation of
this relationship which means as much the events or "signs"
which reveal the mode of existence which this union renews as
the didactic indication of the limits and presuppositions of
God's union with man.

When the Church in the Eucharist lives the miracle of life
freed from every natural necessity, then the miracles of Christ
which the gospel narrative recounts are nothing but particular
manifestations and details of this miracle itself. If the initial
miracle is true – if the created can exist in the mode of the
uncreated – then no other miracle is impossible, then "the
limits of nature are conquered", the limitations and necessities
which govern the created are lifted. Then "the blind see again,
the lame walk, lepers are cleansed, deaf hear, the dead are
raised" (Lk 7.22). For the Church, the gospel narratives of the
miracles of Christ were never apologetic proofs which coerce
reason and demand faith in the divine-humanity of Christ.
But they were "signs", signs which point to that event which
the Church experiences every time "in the breaking of the
bread": Life becomes imperishable and the mortal immortal in
a manner "most becoming of God".

h. Willing death

Christ unites in his Person the divine and human natures. As God, he is the one "incarnate for us". As man, he is the one who "has died and risen". The incarnation of God without the resurrection of man, the removal of death, would be a defective truth, a theophany rather indifferent to man – unrelated in any way with the existential adventure of every man, his life and death.

The Church experiences the mystery of the death and resurrection of Christ as a way and manner which every man assumes who participates in the divine life, immortality and incorruptibility. We speak of a "way" and "manner" and we must try to say, even in the conventional concepts of our everyday language, what we mean.

The death of Christ was a willing death – "he gave himself up" (Eph 5.25). His death was not the unavoidable termination of the created nature, which the existential event tends to bring about with only its own functions, and which is led gradually to the weakening and to the final extinction of its psychosomatic activities. Christ gave himself up to death forsaking totally every tendency and aspiration for physical self-existence of the created and transposed the event of existence and life into a relationship with the Father, into his abandonment to the will of the Father, into the surrender of his "spirit" "into the hands" of the Father.

We die because after the fall it is our created nature which gives existence to our hypostasis or ego; we draw existence from the possibilities or energies of our nature which are not able by themselves to sustain self-existence and the principle of life, because they wear out and end at some point. But the hypostasis of Christ draws existence and life not from the human and created, but from his divine and uncreated nature, which exists as the freedom of the Father's will and the response of the Son's love to this will. The birth even of Christ's bodily individuality is not a result of the autonomous impulse for perpetuation of the created nature – "not from blood, nor from the will of the flesh, nor from the will of a husband, but he is born from God" (cf. Jn 1.13). Consequently his supernatural birth, by the standard of the created, alone was sufficient to assure the freedom of Christ's flesh from corruption and death.

But the will of God's love was to transform the necessity of death, which the fall imposed on human nature in general, also into the general possibility of incorruptibility and immortality. Therefore Christ accepts even death willingly, and so he places the final conclusion of man's rebellion within the freedom of love and obedience to the Father's will, that is, within the mode of existence of the uncreated. Hereafter everyone can transform the necessity of death into a freedom of self-renunciation from every demand of self-existence; everyone can repeat the movement of Christ, a movement opposite to Adam's rebellion and repose the possibility of existence no longer in mortal nature, but in the personal relationship with the Father. In the person of Christ, human nature is granted the same relationship of life with God which the Son has with the Father – and this is the meaning of the "adoption" on which Paul insists (Eph 1.5; Gal 4.5). Now, from the willing "destruction" of life "we save" life (Mt 16.25), "dying with" Christ "we live together with" him (2 Tim 2.11) forever. This is the meaning of the "discipline" which the Church defines as an imitation of the cross of Christ, this is the testimony of the martyrs who remain "examples" for the Church and give significance to its discipline: Life is not biological survival, but a relationship with God, the denial of the demands for life in itself, the realization of existence as a loving communion.

None of this means that for Christ death was exempt from the pain and horror which every human creature has at the uncoupling of this hypostasis from the way in which nature gives effect existentially to this hypostasis. Christ did not simply die, but summarized in his death all the tragedy which can be heaped up by man's sin, the existential failure and missing the mark of his nature: His fellow people repaid him hatred and death, they who received from him only love and kindness. They killed him with violence and degradation, in the way in which criminals were executed, those who are especially unsuccessful in human society. They put him up between two robbers, like a criminal himself. He died with the martyr death of the cross – a death of extreme pain when the body, no longer tolerating to be supported on the wounds of the nails in order to raise the chest and to draw breath, surrenders to suffocation and choking. "And through all these things he showed his love for us."

i **"Ransom" and "redemption"**

The loving self-offering of Christ is a "ransom" for the "redemption" of every human death. Already in the time of the first apostolic community, the Church tried to say and to describe the experience of salvation which Christ's death on the cross had given us. It used the inevitable images and categories of our everyday life, even though our everyday life is subject to the fall. And so in order for us to understand what the Church wants to indicate by means of these images from our fallen experience, we must purify them as much as we can of every individualistic, rationalistic, or utilitarian interpretation, that is from every element that holds life back.

We speak of "adoption", of "reconciliation", of "ransom", of "redemption", of "justification". In our everyday life, these images function subject more to the mentality of relationships of transactions, of individual restoration, of subjective security. But the Church with these same concepts intends to indicate the sacrificial love of God for man, the restoration of the created to the lifegiving relationship with the uncreated, the renunciation of the existential autonomy of the individual, the drawing of life from loving communion. How we are to construe these images is, then, an important question: will it be with meaning they have in the fallen condition or with the meaning they have in the ecclesial perspective?

A great misconception and distortion of the ecclesial truth about the abolition of death by the Cross of Christ had already appeared in the West by the first centuries and progressively dominated the spiritual climate. Tertullian, Augustine, Anselm, and Thomas Aquinas are the great landmarks in the formation and imposition of this distortion which was finally proclaimed as an official teaching of the western Church at the Council of Trent (1545-1563). It is a matter of a legalistic interpretation of the biblical images of "ransom" which Christ paid with his death on the cross seeing that "he redeemed" humanity from slavery and subjection to sin and death – an interpretation adapted to the violent experience of man after the fall.

According to this interpretation, man's sin is a disturbance and violation of the divine "order of justice" and at the same time an offense to the honour and majesty of God. The degree of guilt for this disturbance and offense is measured in proportion to the degree of importance of the one who has been offended – as in human justice. Then the infinite majesty and justice of God demanded an infinite substitute for propitiation. But finite man could not offer such an infinite substitute, even if the whole of humanity were sacrificed to satisfy the divine justice. Therefore, God himself undertook to pay, in the person of his Son, the infinite ransom for the satisfaction of his justice. Christ was punished with the death on the cross in place of sinful humanity and in order that sinful humanity receive expiation. In the teaching of Luther and of Calvin later, it is not simply divine justice, but the *wrath* of God which must be appeased by the sacrifice of Christ on the cross.

The changes which this theory occasioned in the faith of the Church is literally incalculable. It changed the truth of God by subordinating the freedom of his love to the relentless necessity of an egocentric and savage justice which demanded sadistic satisfaction. The God of the Church, from being a Father and "passionate lover" of mankind, was transformed into an implacable judge and menacing avenger whose justice rejoices (according to the view of Augustine) when it sees the sinners who are being tormented in hell.

The successive waves of atheism in the spiritual life of the West in these last centuries, the repeated outbreaks of liberation from the "sadistic God" of the Roman juridical tradition, is not a phenomenon unrelated to this theory of the "satisfaction of divine justice by Christ's death on a cross", just as the joining of Christian truth to the conscience by an unsurpassed weaving of guilt is not unrelated. This theory changes the ecclesial notion of sin as missing the mark and a failure of mankind; it accepts it as a legal transgression and punishable deviation. It is a cause of egocentric guilt and a ground of egocentric justification as well, because the psychic mechanisms of mankind after the fall still need guilt and often provoke it, seeing that by means of an objective and indisputable "redemption" they achieve the egocentric satisfaction of individual "justification". The schema "guilt – redemption – justification" is a typical symptom of every "natural religion", an expression of human psychology which refuses to give up the individualistic version of existence and seeks to defeat death by its own meritorious accomplishments, even strengthened by the exchange value of some transcendent "ransom".

Thus the Church is transformed into a moralistic religion, serving the individual self-assurance of mankind. The Cross of Christ ceases to incarnate and to reveal the core of the gospel of salvation: The renunciation of life in itself, in order that life be achieved, the acceptance of death if the last existential resistance of individuality is to yield and existence is to be drawn not from the created nature, but from the personal relationship with God the Father, the giver of life.

If the Cross of Christ became the symbol par excellence of the Church, a sensible expression and manifestation of the faith of Christians, it was not simply in order to recall the passion of the God-man and the price which was paid to the enraged justice of God. Christians impressed the sign of the cross on their bodies, revealing the willing self-renunciation of individual self-sufficiency, the sacrificial offering of their life to the will of the Father. "All visible things need a cross," said St Maximus the Confessor, "and all intelligible things need a tomb."[9] Everything that can be seen, everything which becomes accessible to us by means of individual senses and every knowledge which we acquire by our individual understanding, everything which seems to be subordinated to us

---

[9]"Chapters on Knowledge", § 67 in *Maximus Confessor: Selected Writings*, tr. George C. Berthold (New York, 1985) p. 140.

thanks to our individual abilities, must be crucified and buried, be put to death as individual certainties and a fortress of the ego, if they are to function as a loving relationship and self-transcendence.

Therefore Christians sign their bodies with the sign of the cross, not only when they pray, but "when they begin any deed whatever";[10] "over bread to be eaten, and over cups from which to drink, on coming in and on going out ... when going to bed and when rising again".[11] Every phase and every turn of our everyday life is sealed with the mark of lifegiving death, of obedience to the will of the Father, the will of life, because the Cross is not a sign of recollection and emotional or morally instructive reference, but a symbol and manifestation of conformation to Christ's mode of existence, the way of life. As such a symbol revealing the life which constitutes the Church and the hope of the faithful, the cross is impressed finally even on the tombs of those who have fallen asleep, affirming their entry into the "land of the living".

j. The Risen One

Christ rose again on the third day after his burial. Both the biblical testimonies and the church's later iconography and hymnology allude to the resurrection indirectly, one could say, by means of signs like the empty tomb, the angel of God who freed the entrance of the grave, the linen burial clothes "lying by themselves". A particular moment when the dead body of Christ received life again and began to function biologically again is neither specified nor described as in the case of the dead whom Christ himself raised during the period of his public life. But there is the experience and evidence of his bodily appearances after the resurrection: The risen Christ appears to the myrrh-bearing women and to the travellers on the road to Emmaus and to the gathering of the disciples in the upper room in Jerusalem or on the shores of Lake Tiberias.

For the experience and certainty of the Church, the resurrection of Christ differs from the resurrections of the dead

[10] Origen, *Commentary on Ezekiel*, 9.4. P.G. 13, 801A.
[11] St Cyril of Jerusalem, *Catachetical Lectures*, 13.36.

which he himself realized in his earthly life. To the dead body of Lazarus, or of the son of the widow of Nain, or the daughter of Jairus, the sovereign command of Christ restores the dead functions of life, just as in the cases of other miracles he restored certain specific functions, the sight of the blind or the hearing and speech of the man deaf and dumb or of walking to the paralytic – but, the bodies of those raised remained corruptible and mortal. All of them died again at some later time because their bodies which had once been raised were subject, as they were before they were raised, to the consequences of the human fall, to the necessity of corruption and death. The raisings of the dead which are described in the Holy Scripture are, to the human eye, astonishing examples of the power of God, that is, of his freedom from every natural limitation. This power can overturn the *laws* of nature but cannot change the *mode of existence* of nature. Such a change cannot be imposed from without; it can only be the fruit of personal freedom, an accomplishment of freedom. As we have often emphasized in the previous pages, it is the person who hypostasizes life and existence, and hypostasizes it either as a natural self-sufficiency (subordinating existence to the necessities of the created) or as an event of loving relationship and erotic communion with God (freeing existence from corruption and death). But love and eros are not imposed from without; they are only an achievement of personal freedom.

This achievement of freedom is completed by Christ on the Cross and is manifest existentially in his resurrection. By his obedience to the Father's will even to the point of death, Christ leads his human nature to the perfect renunciation of every demand for existential self-sufficiency, transposing the existence of nature into the relationship of love and freedom of obedience to God. And this nature which draws its existence from the relationship with God does not die because, even though created, it exists now in the manner of the uncreated, not in the manner of the created. Christ's raised body is a material body, a created nature. But it differs from the bodies of other raised people because it exists now in the mode of the uncreated, the mode of freedom from every natural necessity. And so, while it is sensible and tangible, with flesh and bones

(Lk 24.30), while it can take nourishment like all other bodies (and the risen Christ eats honey and fish before the eyes of his disciples (Lk 24.42)) and while the marks of the wounds which he received are obvious on him, still this same body enters the upper room "with the doors locked" (Jn 20.1) and vanishes at Emmaus after the breaking of the bread (Lk 24.31) and finally is received into heaven (Mk 16.19; Lk 24.51) enthroning the human "clay" in the glory of the divine life.

The transformation in the mode of existence of Christ's human nature after his resurrection is shown in the Gospels indirectly again: it is not possible to define and describe it with the objective categories which determine our common everyday experiences. It notes an "otherness": he is the well-known "son of man", but "in a different form" (Mk 16.12). Mary Magdalene in the garden with his tomb in it thought him to be a gardener. The two travellers on the road to Emmaus thought him a chance passer-by. The disciples who were fishing in Lake Tiberias heard him asking them for something "good to eat" and did not suspect again that it was he who was waiting for them on the shore. Everyone discovered him suddenly and self-evidently, but after they had been mistaken at the beginning. What is it that made him different in principle and which had to be transcended in order to recognize him? Certainly something which is not to be said but only experienced. Perhaps if the relationship with him stops at the apparent individual, it will not succeed in recognizing the hypostasis freed from individual self-sufficiency. We do not know and we cannot describe the experience; we can only dare to approach it interpretively from the events which accompany it: The body of the risen Christ is the human nature free from every limitation and every need. It is a human body with flesh and bones, but which does not draw life from its biological functions, but is hypostasized in a real existence thanks to the personal relationship with God which alone constitutes it and gives it life.

k. The general resurrection

Christ "raised the whole race of Adam when he rose from the grave" – the whole race, every one. The experiences of individualistic fallen life impede us from understanding this existential relationship of one man with the whole humanity, of one person with the nature in general: How is the entire human nature cut off from the possibility of life in the person of Adam, and how in the person of Christ is the whole nature again "reconstituted" and given life? Our philosophical categories can at least help in understanding this event which is, however, a pivot and foundation for approaching the truth of sin and salvation, a presupposition for finding meaning in the tragedy of history.

"For as in Adam all die, so also in Christ shall all be made alive;" "for as by a man came death, by a man has come also the resurrection of the dead" (1 Cor 15.22, 21 *RSV*). The Apostle Paul insists on the inclusion of the entire nature in one person, but the way in which or how this is accomplished, he indicates only with images. He speaks of the "dividing wall of hostility" which has been broken down in the flesh of Christ (Eph 2.14), of the "wild olive tree" which has been grafted onto the "cultivated olive tree" (Rom 11.24). Nevertheless, his insistence on the abolition of death "through death" – to which the Church returns ceaselessly – permits us to articulate an attempt at interpretation, beyond the symbolism of the images: We may say, given the inadequacy of our language, that the personal freedom of Christ, accepting death willingly, leads human nature to the total renunciation of every demand of self-existence. And since each human death is the obligatory and given elimination of the individual's existential autonomy, the love of God accepts each death in the way in which he accepted the sacrifice of his incarnate Son, as a removal of the resistance of the created to his reception by God.

Thus, in the person of Christ, risen and ascended "in the flesh", God receives "all flesh", when he lays down in death the demands of his self-existence; God is united with every one and gives him life. The death which was the "last enemy"

(1 Cor 15.26) is proved now to be a triumph of the love of God, an entry into life. Therefore, "we would rather be away from the body and at home with the Lord ... we know that while we are at home in the body we are away from the Lord ... For we know that if the earthly tent we live in is destroyed, we have a building from God, a house not made with hands, eternal in the heavens" (2 Cor 5.1-8 *RSV*).

But first, that "what is mortal may be swallowed up by life" in death (2 Cor 5.4), every willing renunciation by man of his existential automony functions for the love of God as a repetition and imitation of the self-renunciation on the cross of the Son, because the flesh itself which we wear, even if it continues to draw existence and life from its biological functions, is the same nature as the flesh of the risen Christ who participates in the life of the Trinity. In his person our common nature has the same relationship with God as the Son has with the Father. And the love of the Father for his incarnate Son is not a sentiment or subjective experience, but a lifegiving activity bestowing essence, constitutive of what exists. Therefore, when our individual flesh lays aside unwillingly (in death) or willingly (in baptism, spiritual discipline or martyrdom) the resistence of its self-existence, our created hypostasis is united with the current of life which flows through our nature after its hypostatic union with the Divinity in the person of Christ. Just as, then, the love of God created all things "through the Word", even so "through the incarnate Word" he renews all things and makes them incorruptible.

1. The "eighth day"

The Church looks for "the resurrection of the dead and the life of the world to come". This world of corruption and death will at some point in time complete its existential cycle, not in order to sink down into the non-existence from which it proceeded, but in order that it appear "in another form" – in order that the risen flesh of Christ be disclosed in its general, cosmic dimensions, that the world reveal the flesh of God, "that God may be all in all" (1 Cor 15.28).

This will be the "eighth day" of creation: In opposition to the "week which measures time", the eighth day "indicates the mode of the condition beyond nature and time".[12] It will be a time no longer of perishable succession, but a perfecting loving relationship which is fulfilled unceasingly in a dynamic transformation "from glory to glory" (2 Cor 3.18). Whatever we say now about this future glory will be only a dim portrait of that reality. "For now we see in a mirror dimly, but then face to face" (1 Cor 13.12 *RSV*).

In the dimensions of the "eighth day", the reality of the Resurrection, the union of God with "the whole race of Adam" is revealed, his union with all men without exception. But this union, while it will abolish man's natural distance from God, will not violate, not even then, the freedom of each person. And so, for those who are "worthy", as St Maximus says, who accept the love of God, the union with Him will be a "divine and inconceivable pleasure", while for those who are "unworthy", those who have rejected the possibility of love, it will be "unspeakable grief".[13] No other quality of life exists on the "eighth day": love judges, love justifies.

Until then we have a foretaste of what we look for within the limits of the Church, the limits of the dynamic "leaven" which prepares the stuff of the world for the perfection of the "eighth day". The body of the Church is the "beginning" and the "pledge" of the future glory. There we live by sharing our nourishment and life, by transforming individual survival into a loving relationship (with the Eucharist, spiritual discipline, worship) – we exist with the name that the Church gives us, indicative of our personal hypostasis, and with which the saints love us, the Mother of God, Christ. We do not separate living and dead; we offer our Eucharist in common to God, because what makes us exist is his own love – even before the general resurrection the love of God constitutes and gives life to the existence of us all, of the living and the dead: "None of us lives to himself, and none of us dies to himself. If we live,

---

[12]Maximus Confessor, *Chapters on Theology* 1.51, P.G. 90, 1101C.
[13]Ibid. 4.20, P.G. 90, 1312C.

we live to the Lord, and if we die, we die to the Lord; so then, whether we live or whether we die, we are the Lord's" (Rom 14.7-8 *RSV*).

What is the way in which the hypostasis of the dead, even though a created nature, is given effect and lives before the general resurrection? In what way was the human hypostasis preserved before the incarnation of Christ and his descent among the dead? How was and is the freedom of our personal hypostases expressed after the dissolution of biological individuality? All these questions receive their answer not with logical propositions which do not go beyond the possibilities of empirical verification, but with the movement of our trust and self-surrender to the love of God. Our individual understanding confirms our individual approach to life, the individual way of existence. Faith in God is a change in the mode of existence, and therefore the language of faith is not related to individual comprehension, individual intellectual self-sufficiency. It is a language hymning the love of God, a language invoking his mercy. His own love founds our personal hypostasis "through an excess of passionate love" and the passionate lover will never abandon his beloved to non-existence. Without recognition and acceptance of this divine love, death is just a shocking and inexplicable absurdity. But on the contrary, for the faithful it is the last and extreme test of their trust and self-surrender to God, to God who "calls into existence the things that do not exist" (Rom 4.17).

9

The Church

a. Called – gathered

The first community of Christ's disciples appear in history with the name "ecclesia".[1] By this word it declared its identity and its truth.

"Ecclesia" (from a Greek verb "to call out") means the gathering which is a result of a call or invitation. It is a gathering or assembling of those called. The first disciples of Christ had the consciousness that they were "called", called by him to an assembly of unity, to an ecclesia. Not to be faithful to a new "religion", nor to be partisans of a new ideology or social teaching. What united them was not the reception of some theoretical "principles" or "axioms", but the reception of the call which radically changed their lives: It transformed individuals, detached units, into a single body, the Church. Their gathering is not exhausted in a simple meeting together; it is not a passing, casual event. They live as a church, as a single body of life, they share life as "brothers" – just like brothers who draw their existence from the same womb – they are "members" of an organic, living "body".

The people of Israel expressed a certain analogous self-consciousness in its history. It did not represent a "religion" either, be it the correct or the best of all others. It was, above all, a people of those who had been "called": a people whom the "living God" – known by immediate historical experience

---

[1]"Ecclesia" is translated "church" which is itself derived from the Greek word, "kyriakos", meaning "belonging to the Lord". In this passage which refers to the etymology, "ecclesia" is retained. – tr.

– had called to realize a concrete mission. Not theoretical confidence or religious beliefs, but God's call gathered and unified the twelve tribes of Israel into one, chosen people, bound in its relation to God by a "Covenant". This consciousness is expressed in the word "synagogue" which signifies the assembling of the Israelite community. "Synagogue" as well as "ecclesia" translate the same Hebrew term, "qahal". The two words are differentiated conceptually, however, when the disciples of Christ choose the second for the designation of their own community, handing the first over to the Jews exclusively.

The Church is also this one chosen people, the "new Israel", with a new historical mission: to reveal to the world God's new relationship and covenant with mankind "in Christ Jesus". The unity of this new "people of God" no longer depends at all, on tribal elements. To the contrary, it is a community open "to all nations". It is founded on a new "Covenant" with God, sealed by the blood of Christ's sacrifice on the cross. For you to share in this people, for you to be a member of the body of the Church, is an act of accepting the "New Covenant": the act of "breaking bread" and "blessing the cup", the participation in the Eucharistic meal.

Many people today seem to have forgotten this truth which defines and manifests the Church: the Church is the gathering in the Eucharistic meal. Not a foundation, not a religious institution, not a governing hierarchy, not buildings and offices and organizational arrangement. It is the people of God gathered in the "breaking of the bread" and the "blessing of the cup". It is the children of God who are scattered abroad" (Jn 11.52 *RSV*) who are gathered now in the unity of life of the ecclesial body. In the Acts of the Apostles we have the first record of this initial foundation which constitutes and makes up the Church: Those who believe in the preaching of the Apostles, assemble and "devote themselves to the teaching and the fellowship and to the breaking of bread" (2.42) – "all who believed were together … and day by day, attending the temple together, and breaking bread in their homes, they partook of food with rejoicing" (2.44,46 *RSV*, mod.).

b. Paschal meal

But the Eucharistic meal which constitutes and reveals the Church is not a theoretically determined institution in which Christ's disciples are historically innovative. Just as Christ himself assumed the given human flesh renewing what was assumed, so his Church assumed the historical flesh of the time transforming what it assumed.

The Eucharistic meal is a consequence and extension of the passover meal of the Jews. "Passover" for the Jews means a passing, a crossing. It was the greatest festival of the year, the remembrance of the crossing of the Red Sea, the celebration of the deliverance of Israel from slavery to the Pharaohs, from their captivity in Egypt. Every year on the eve of the feast, in the evening, the Jewish family would gather in a festival dinner. At some point during this dinner, the eldest member of the family took a cup with wine into his hands to propose a toast. The toast was a prayer to God: the Thanksgiving.[2] He would thank God for what he had given and promised to the fathers of Israel and to all his people, but especially for the miraculous crossing of the Red Sea and their salvation from the Egyptians. Then he would drink first and pass the cup from hand to hand so that all could drink and participate in this way in the Thanksgiving.

Christ celebrated this passover meal of the Jews with his disciples on the eve of his death on the cross, in the upper room in Jerusalem. But no longer for the remembrance and reliving of God's Old Covenant with his people and of the miraculous confirmation of the Lord's faithfulness to this Covenant. Christ gives a new content to the passover meal, the content of the New Covenant. Now the Passover is not a passage of only one people from captivity to freedom, but a crossing of the whole race of men from death to life. "In the flesh" of Christ and "in his blood" the "dividing wall of hostility" between the created and the uncreated is abolished. Now the created can exist in the manner of the uncreated, the way of "true life".

The flesh and blood of Christ are a world, a creation, but not the world and the creation in the rebellion of self-existence. It

[2] In Greek, "Eucharist". – tr.

is the created existence as a reference and offering to God, as an affirmation of thanksgiving to the lifegiving love of the Father. The food of the eucharistic dinner of the Church – bread and wine – are also the creation as a reference and offering to God, in accord with the example of the mode of existence of Christ's flesh. The Church receives the world under the forms of bread and wine – forms comprehensive of every food and possibility of human life – and offers it to God. It refers and offers the life of the created to the will of the Father's love and gives thanks for the existential possibility of reference which has been realized in Christ.

"Do this in remembrance of me," Christ said to his disciples sharing the bread and wine on the evening of the Last Supper (Lk 22.19). Remembrance means in the Scripture, not simply going back over something in the memory, the recollection of past events, but the reliving and renewal of a relationship, of an event of life. The communion of bread and wine of the Eucharist is the reliving and renewal of that relationship with the uncreated which was realized "in the flesh and blood" of Christ. The bread and wine of the Eucharist are not neutral objects which serve for the nourishment and survival of the mortal individual, but they are the creation which is communicated and received as a lifegiving relationship with the Father, they are what is created in a unity of life with the uncreated, they are the Body and Blood of Christ, just as he himself affirms: "Take, eat. This is my body. All of you drink of this. This is my blood."

c. Renewal of life

The Church is a meal, an action of eating and drinking. Eating and drinking are the presupposition for the life of man, the way he shares in life. The distortion of life and the entry of death into the world happened with an act of eating as well – eating of the fruit "of the tree of the knowledge of good and evil". The first man separated the taking of nourishment – the possibility of life – from communion and relationship with God. He took nourishment for himself alone, for the maintenance of his individuality; he wanted to realize life not as communion and relationship, but as individual natural survival and self-existence.

In the Eucharistic meal, the Church realizes an approach to life radically opposed to that of those who were first formed. She takes nourishment not within the framework of the individual demand for life, but in order to realize life as a reference to God and communion with him. This change in the manner of realizing life is neither simply an ethical obedience to commands, nor an emotional elevation or mystical experience. It is the action of eating and drinking which is transformed into a loving co-inherence of life, into a denial of the rebellion of self-existence. Our sharing in the Eucharistic meal is a communion with our brothers and with God – we communicate in life, we agree to exist only by loving and being loved. Therefore the ecclesial Eucharist proves to be an image and manifestation of the triadic mode of existence, a revelation of "true life", of the Kingdom of God.

Precisely since the realization and manifestation of the Kingdom of God in the Eucharist is neither an ethical accomplishment or simply a mystical experience, it surpasses, therefore, the possibilities of human achievement. It is a gift, an expression of grace, a reshaping of life, a renewal of the possibilities of life. The gift has been given to us and is given to us "in the flesh and blood" of Christ, with the real union of created and uncreated. But our existence itself, the otherness of our person, is not our own achievement, but a gift and expression of grace, and so also the making our mortal life incorruptible, the change of the mode of our existence. God, the Holy Spirit of God, is a lifegiving power and principle; he grants existence, founds our personal hypostasis as an existential answer to the call of his passionate love, and he renews our createdness building the "new man" – the union of Divinity and humanity – "in the flesh" of Christ.

The renewal of the life of the created by the intervention of the Spirit, the Comforter, is a presupposition for the constitution of the Church and our sharing in the Church. When we speak about renewal of life, we do not mean either the ethical "improvement" of man, or his legal "restoration", but an event as real as the constitution of our life itself, the composition of the created. The teaching of Christ to his disciples or the repetition and imitation of the Last Supper are not enough to constitute the "new creation" of the Church. It was necessary that the life giving "descent" of the Spirit of God on human flesh occur – just as the Spirit "descended" on the Virgin in order for the incarnation of Christ to take place. This intervention of the Comforter which constitutes the "new flesh" was experienced historically by the Church on the day of Pentecost. It is also experienced in every Eucharistic meal in the living change of bread and wine into Body and Blood of Christ. The same intervention is also the beginning of the participation of each of us in the Church within the event of Baptism.

d. Pentecost

After the Resurrection and Ascension of Christ, the widest group of his disciples – "the company of persons was in all about a hundred and twenty" – "with one accord devoting themselves to prayer and petition" (Acts 1.14-15) in the upper room in Jerusalem. But this gathering did not yet constitute a *Church*. It was an assembling of people who brought together common memories and common hopes, frightened people, without a clear awareness of what it was to which they devoted themselves and for what work they had been called. A few days before, they had asked their Teacher if within this year he would free the Jewish people from the yoke of the Romans and re-establish the Kingdom of Israel (Acts 1.6). Even after the experience of the Resurrection, their expectations seem not to have transcended the limits of worldly programs and ambitions.

These people and their assembly were transformed radically by the event of Pentecost. Luke tries to describe for us the experience of that day using images which can form a certain analogy: They were again "all together in one place" – gathered in the well-known upper room in Jerusalem. "And suddenly a sound came from heaven like the rush of a mighty wind, and it filled all the house where they were sitting" (Acts 2.1-2) – something like the noise of a strong wind which seemed to come from above and to fill the place where the disciples were gathered. And with some kind of visual experience, as if burning tongues were divided – "tongues as of fire" – on the gathered disciples, "and they were all filled with the Holy Spirit".

But if the experience of these events can be formulated only with analogical images, the transformation which was accomplished in the disciples with their "filling" by the Holy Spirit has very definite manifestations perceptible to all: They "began to speak in other tongues" – they suddenly began to speak in all the languages of the peoples and tribes who had gathered in Jerusalem for the feast of Pentecost. Each of the crowd heard his own dialect from the mouth of the disciples, "and they were amazed and wondered". These disciples, terrified until then, simple men, not intellectuals – "uneducated, common men", as Luke notes – began to preach to the crowds "the mighty works of God", with the ease and wisdom of very experienced speakers. Now at last they knew what it was and what they had been promised, they knew the meaning of the events which had preceded and to what perspective of life they were calling men by their preaching. They called them to be baptized in order that they themselves receive "the gift of the Holy Spirit" – participate in the possibility of Pentecost, now always open. And they gathered the "three thousand" who were baptized that first day to the table of the Eucharist – "to the breaking of bread". At the same time, "many signs and wonders were done through the apostles" – healing of sick people, curing of those possessed, and even the raising of the dead, such as Tabitha in Joppa.

The descent of the Holy Spirit is not a magical addition of abilities and gifts to man. It is a liberation of the possibilities of life which has nothing unreasonable and "supernatural" in it. The Spirit descends on our nature transforming not the principle of nature (which is our nature), but the mode of its existence, the mode of the composition of our hypostasis. Receiving the Spirit of God, we cease to exist by drawing our hypostasis from the necessity of biological succession and autonomous individuality. We exist, since the will of God's love gives life and constitutes and hypostasizes our being. This freedom from natural necessity and the harmonization of our existence with the lifegiving will of God has as an organic result all the "signs" which the Scripture refers to the life of Christ and the Apostles – "signs" which the Church lives unceasingly in the persons of her saints.

Healing the sick and speaking in tongues and theological wisdom and every other gift are the fruit of man's rebirth "in the Holy Spirit". Just as the first manifestations of life in the birth of man are wonderful and astonishing, the first breath and the first cry, and later the first smile and the expression in the look and the first words which the baby articulates – wonderful, but also self-evident manifestations of the personality which has been born, in the same way the fruits of the rebirth of man "in the Holy Spirit" are wonderful, but also self-evident. If these fruits do not always become apparent, it is not because the Spirit is granted with quantitative differentiations – "for it is not by measure that he gives the Spirit" (Jn 3.34 *RSV*) – but because the resistance of death which our freedom develops is differentiated in some way.

e. Existential transformation

Pentecost – the descent of the Holy Spirit – is the foundational and constitutive event of the Church. An institution is not founded, but the "new creation of Grace" is born, the possibility of immortal life given by God to man. Therefore even Pentecost – the descent of the Holy Spirit – is not an event which has been completed "once for all time", but the event which always and continuously constitutes and forms the Church.

The Church is a Meal, an act of eating and drinking. But in order to grant life (and not to serve a transitory survival), this eating and drinking presupposes the lifegiving activity of the Holy Spirit, the transformation of perishable food into the food of imperishability, into a possibility of eternal life, into a "medicine of immortality". In every eucharistic gathering, the Church invokes the Holy Spirit of God in order to complete this existential transformation: "Send down your Holy Spirit on us and on these gifts before us. And make this bread to be the precious Body of your Christ, and what is in this cup to be the precious Blood of your Christ, changing them by your Holy Spirit". And the community gathered around the Table confirm the invocation with the exclamation of affirmation, "Amen". This small word, the "yes" of man's freedom in the love of God, as a liturgical expression is the collective binding to the Covenant, the integral joining to and blessing by that in which one is hypostasized. The affirmation of the eucharistic community to the invocation of the Holy Spirit happens "in Christ" who is "the amen, the faithful and true witness" (Rev 3.14): "For all the promises of God find their Yes in him. That is why we utter the Amen through him, to the glory of God" (2 Cor 1.20 *RSV*). We seek the Spirit from the Father offering the "amen" which is Christ himself, the perfect obedience to the divine will of life.

The existential change which is completed by the descent of the Holy Spirit in the Eucharist refers neither to objects in themselves nor to individuals in themselves, but to the relationship of individuals with the objects, a relationship of reference and offering of creation to God by man, a relationship which transfigures the mode of life changing the existence both of individuals and of things in the eucharistic communion with God into participation in the triadic fullness of life. We call down the Holy Spirit "on us *and* on these gifts before us" seeking precisely the transformation of life, that life be made imperishable, that the gifts be changed and that those who share in the gifts share in a new creation, freed from death – in the Body of Christ.

What is transformed by the lifegiving descent of the Spirit is not the nature of individuals and of things, but the mode of existence of the nature. Man remains a created nature; the same is true of the gifts offered. But this created nature is offered to exist and be permitted to exist by drawing its life not from its own vital possibilities (which are transitory and perishable) but by reference to and surrender to the love of God and by communion with him – as the created flesh of the uncreated Word, the Body and Blood of Christ. Christ was incarnate, not in appearance only, not on the level of sentimental and ethical analogies, but in the way in which human flesh is created and survives. So, man in the Eucharist offers to God, not his emotions or his moral accomplishments, but the way in which his life is realized: the taking of nourishment which maintains him in existence. He offers his nourishment, his life, which means: he does not claim it for his own, but recognizes it as a gift of God's love – "your own of your own we offer you". This offering meets the lifegiving reply of the Holy Spirit, who changes the manner in which life is maintained into a way of imperishability of life. Thus man's nourishment – bread and wine – is raised in the Eucharist to a possibility of eternal life, that is, of a unity of the created with the uncreated: it is raised and shown to be an event of life identified with the cosmic flesh of God the Word, the Body and Blood of Christ. What is completed in the ecclesial Eucharist is what was completed with the Spirit's "coming upon" the Mother of God, what will be perfected in the entire creation when "all things are summed up in Christ" (Eph 1.10): The created is united with the uncreated, bread and wine are the Body and Blood of Christ, the ecclesial gathering a realization and manifestation of the Kingdom of God.

f. "Transubstantiation" and "symbol"

The Christian West has never managed to express life with a language freed from intellectual schemata, from the need to define "objective realities". It has refused the dynamic of life, remaining attached to the "objectivity" of concepts and essences. It has always defined existence by the objective properties of essence – it has proved impossible for western people to understand how two different essences or natures (the created and the uncreated) can have a common mode of existence. Therefore, they have not even been able to see the ecclesial Eucharist as an existential event, precisely as a change of the mode of existence, which does not entail also a change of the essence or nature.

And so, the Roman Catholics have spoken of the *transubstantiation* of the bread and wine of the Eucharist: The forms offered (the bread and wine) are transubstantiated, they change essence, their nature is transformed. "Through the blessing of the bread and the wine the whole essence of the bread is transformed into the essence of the body of Christ and the whole essence of the wine into the essence of his blood",[3] while the perceptible marks of the bread and the wine remain only in appearance, being transformed into "external accidents".

Nevertheless, this essential change has no relationship with the existential event, the human adventure of life and death – it does not touch and it does not elucidate the mode of life, the corruptible or the incorruptible, the mortal or the immortal. It is an intellectually defined and emotionally believed "supernatural" (finally magical) change of the nature of the objects – just as the salvation of the individual who approaches the communion of the transubstantiated elements is "supernatural" (finally magical). The Eucharist does not transform the mode of existence of man – it does not change the individual mode into an ecclesial and triadic mode. Therefore the Church is not identified with the Eucharist and the Kingdom, but the Church is changed simply into an institutional framework where the individual "becomes familiar" with the supernatural transubstantiation. Thus, Roman Catholicism introduces and promotes an individualistic religiosity, like the distinction between the Church from the body of the laity, her identification merely with the administrative hierarchy – in radical antithesis with the apostolic truth and manifestation of the Church.

A natural consequence of this is the attempt of Roman Catholics to dematerialize as much as possible the offered gifts of the Eucharist, since they represent symbolically the completed transubstantiation. The bread of the Eucharist is not the everyday bread of people; they have replaced it with "hosts", an unleavened, almost transparent preparation. And they deprive the laity of sharing in the cup, because the taste of the wine is dangerously opposed to the idea of transubstantiation.

---

[3]Council of Trent, Session XIII, *Decretum de s.s. Eucharistia*, cap. 4. Denz. (36th ed.), tr 1642.

The idea of transubstantiation was thrown out from the first moment by Protestantism, but with the same western attitude of adherence to the "objectivity" of essences. For the Protestants, it is not possible for the essence or nature of the elements of the Eucharist to change; the bread remains in essence bread and the wine remains wine. However, we communicate in the body and blood of Christ, because the bread and the wine function as types, symbols and images, or as a means, an instrument and a token of "spiritual" reception and communion of the faithful with Christ. Here the language becomes completely unrelated to the existential event and the reality of life: Christ is present in the Eucharist, not with his bodily essence which remains in heaven, but only with his lifegiving power which is imparted exclusively to those who approach the Eucharist with faith. Those who do not have faith at their disposal, communicate in simple bread and wine and even "to their condemnation".

So, in place of a "supernatural" transubstantiation, Protestantism introduces an intellectually more secure flight into individual experience – reinforcing isolation in individualistic religiosity. The truth of the Church becomes abstract and secondary, since communion with Christ by means of the Eucharist is an event of subjective readiness and faith – it does not even assume an institutional bearer or mediator for the change in the gifts. The biblical promise of salvation is firmly distinguished from the existential adventure of man; it is reshaped into a legal category of "justification" and experienced as an individual psychological certainty and emotional exaltation, with the ethical "improvement" of character and behaviour as a practical result. The truth of the Triadic God itself, separated from the eucharistic experience of the ecclesial mode of existence, is left as an abstract "dogma", unrelated to the life and hope of man.

g. Mysteries

For the apostolic and patristic tradition and for its historical continuity in Orthodoxy, the Church is realized and revealed in the event of Pentecost, and the event of Pentecost is completed and experienced in every Eucharistic gathering.

The whole life of the faithful, every turn of his life, is a preparation for participation in or an event of participation in the gifts of the Holy Spirit, in the refashioning of life. This refashioning has its dynamic beginning in the act of entry into the Church, in the act by which we become members of the ecclesial body – in Baptism and Chrismation.

We become members of the Church, not by accepting theoretical principles and axioms or ethical obligations, but above all by a bodily act: the triple immersion in and emersion from the water of Baptism, a practical, perceptible conformation to the death and resurrection of Christ. The person who approaches the Church is "buried" as the "former man" and is "raised" by the triple rising up to the Triadic Original. This "burial" is voluntary, in accordance with the example of Christ, a beginning of imperishability of the created and not its dissolution and disappearance. And it comes about within water which is a symbol and womb of life, a constitutive beginning of nature endowed with life.

The first life emerged from water, the first – unimaginable for the mind – differentiation of nature endowed with life from lifeless matter. And from the water of Baptism, new life emerges, the radical differentiation of the personal hypostasis from the individual survival held within the limits of death. The Bishop or Presbyter of the eucharistic body invokes the lifegiving activity of the Holy Spirit in order to change the perceptible form of burial and resurrection into an existential event: "Strip away his old self and renew him in eternal life and fill him with the power of the Holy Spirit in union with your Christ so that he be no longer a child of the body but a child of your kingdom."

The Holy Spirit of God effects in the perceptible data of natural life the change in the mode of existence, the grafting of the perishable into imperishability. In opposition to natural birth which brings a biological unit to life subject to the necessity of progressive decay and death, Baptism *regenerates* existence (1 Pt 1.3) in a named personal otherness which subsists as an hypostasis of life thanks to communion and relationship with the love of the Father. Man ceases to be simply an individual form, just a link in biological succession, a unit of a whole. He is enrolled in the fellowship of the saints, the triadic realization of life. Each of us takes the name of a saint; he realizes dynamically in his person the revelation of God's love.

In the first Church, the Apostles "laid their hands on those who had been baptized and they received the Holy Spirit" (Acts 8.17). This personal transmission of the gifts of the Holy Spirit to the faithful reborn by Baptism is continued within the Church with Chrismation.

By Chrismation the one approaching the Church shares, not only in the basic possibilities of the new regenerated creation of the body of Christ, but is sealed with the seal of personal adoption, a seal of a personal and unique relationship with the Holy Trinity by means of the personal presence of the Holy Spirit in the secret depths of his existence, the core of his hypostasis.

The anointing happens now, not with the laying on of hands, but with aromatic oil in the way in which they anointed the kings of Israel in the Old Testament. The anointing of the kings did not have as a result a change in nature, but in the relationship of the anointed person with the whole body of the people: In the otherness of the royal person the people saw the centre and pivot of their life as communion and unity, and at the same time they saw in him the model of the expected Messiah who is the special "Christ of the Lord", he who frees and re-establishes life in the fullness of God's promises. Similarly, in the personal otherness of each anointed person, the Church sees a new possibility for the true life of the gifts of the Spirit to be realized and revealed together with the image of Christ which frees and re-establishes life in the fullness of the mode of divine life.

The Eucharist, Baptism, Chrismation, are the ways by which the continuing event of Pentecost is realized and made manifest, the descent of the Holy Spirit constitutive of the Church. It has become the custom for us to call these ways *mysteries.*[4] They are not limited to the three referred to above, but are completed with Confession, Priesthood, Marriage, Unction. They are seven specific possibilities of organic enrolment or of dynamic re-enrolment of our individual life in the life of the ecclesial body. At the same time they are events which realize and reveal the Church, a charismatic constituting of the new creation which is given life by the Spirit.

If we use the Greek word "mystery" for these events, it is not in order to attribute a concealed character to them, but in order to show that the enrolling and dynamic approach to the life of the Church is not exhausted in the phenomenology of perceptible symbols. Our conventional language of everyday understanding and of scientific relativity is not enough to define it. It presupposes the general experiential participation of man in order to attain the knowledge of the possibilities of life which are celebrated within the Church.

With the western institutional and bureaucratic understanding of the Church, when we say mysteries today, many people understand formal liturgical acts by which the clergy transmit to the faithful a certain "supernatural" (and finally magical) grace or justification or worthiness or abstract "blessing". After all that we have referred to above, it seems rather superfluous to emphasize that such an understanding is completely unrelated to the life and dynamic regeneration of life, incorruptibility and immortality which the Holy Spirit of God grants by constituting the Church.

h. The ecclesiastical hierarchy

With the same western understanding, many people today identify the Church only with the clergy, that is, the Bishops, Presbyters and Deacons, separating the body of the people from the celebrants of the Church's mysteries. We must see if such a separation can be true, how these positions arise within

[4]The term "mystery" corresponds approximately to the western (Latin) term "sacrament". Nevertheless, in order to recognize a difference of emphasis, Orthodox writers often prefer to retain this Greek term in English. – tr.

the Church, and what relation they have with its truth, the proclamation of "true life".

We will need to return again to our initial definition: Before anything else, the Church is a Meal, the Eucharistic Meal. Just as in the passover meal of the Hebrews, so also in the ecclesial Eucharist there is someone who blesses the cup and sends up the eucharistic prayer – the "eldest" of the family or the "president" of the gathering. Christ had this place of "elder" (or, in Greek, "presbyter") or "president" in the Last Supper on Holy Thursday. After Pentecost, this same place was taken by the Apostles. The Apostles "presided" over the Eucharistic Meal, they sent up the thanksgiving blessing the cup and "breaking the bread". When they were "scattered" on their journeys, to almost every corner of the then known world, they founded Churches "in every city", that is, local eucharistic gatherings where, at least at the beginning, they themselves again "led the Eucharist".

We have enough information from Luke in the "Acts of the Apostles" and also from Paul in his "Letters" about the way the first Christian Churches were founded. The proclamation was, however, the beginning: that is, when one of the Apostles reached a city for the first time, he would visit the Jewish synagogue or the Greek "market" and there he would give a public speech declaring the "new teaching" about the incarnation of God and the salvation of man. Those among the listeners of this first proclamation who showed special interest and wanted to learn more about the new teaching would meet, frequently in private rooms, where the Apostles continued more fully and more analytically the presentation of the truths of the Gospel. In this tighter circle the first believers were prepared for receiving Baptism and the "gift of the Holy Spirit" – to receive them "at the hands of the Apostles" who alone granted them. The baptized formed their eucharistic gathering immediately, that is, their local Church, where the founding Apostle was the president and celebrant.

But the apostolic journey had to be continued, the proclamation of the good news extended to other cities. Its founder obliged, then, to leave the newly constituted Church, would choose one of the faithful to whom, "through the laying on of his hands" again, he granted the distinctive gift to be himself now the president of the local Church, to "preside" at the Eucharist, to perform Baptism, to grant the "gift of the Spirit", to be the spiritual *father* in the work of rebirth and of the "increase in grace and knowledge" of the faithful. In the texts of the New Testament, these first presidents of the particular local Churches are called *Bishops* or *Elders*. The two terms are not differentiated conceptually because the function was not differentiated, indicating that it is a question of one unique president of one single local eucharistic gathering, the local Church.

Nevertheless, from authentic historical evidence of the apostolic period, we gather that there existed from the beginning in each local Church a "council of presbyters", a kind of administrative council which surrounded the president of the local Eucharist.[5] And so, when the number of faithful in a local Church increased significantly and it was finally impossible for them all to meet in one eucharistic gathering, the president had the ability to divide the faithful into particular gatherings by placing one of the presbyters in each one of them. He himself kept the "episcope" of all the particular gatherings, he was the Bishop (*Episcopos*) of the local Church, and the gatherings were "within the limits" of his own jurisdiction – they were particular "parishes". The presbyters celebrated the Eucharist only with an order from the Bishop and in the name of the Bishop, commemorating his name at the moment of the offering of the gifts because he remained as father and grantor of the spiritual gifts being the successor of the Apostles and of Christ.

The distribution of the faithful into particular parishes and the celebration of the Eucharist by the presbyters does not break up the unity of the local Church; it does not take away its character as one Eucharist and one body with the one Bishop as head "in the form and place of Christ". The Bishop is not simply a successor of Christ and of the Apostles with the legal concept of the transfer of rights, nor simply a symbol of the

[5]See the specialized historical study of John Zizioulas, *The Unity of the Church in the Holy Eucharist and the Bishop in the first three Centuries*, Athens 1965 (in Greek).

presence of Christ. The "gift of the Holy Spirit" which he
receives by his ordination renders the Bishop able (beyond his
individual worthiness or unworthiness) to perform the work
of the presence itself of Christ in the Church, to form the
unity of the eucharistic body. And unity for the Church
means, not simply an organizational "connection", "accord"
or "unanimity", but a transformation of the mode of
existence, a change from individual survival to a life of loving
communion, eternal life.

The Bishop "in the form and place of Christ" and the
presbyters "in the form and place" of the Bishop "lead the
Eucharist" – they do not preside over a religious "formal"
worship, it is not the "clergy" who "mediate" and propitiate
the divine: they are the pivots of the unity which transforms
life, they are the "fathers" who "bear" people to immortality
and imperishability. Life is unified and communicated actu-
ally, as in a family. It is not accidental that the first Church
expressed the bonds of the eucharistic community with the
terms which express the bonds of family life: the president of
the Eucharist is "father" and the members of the eucharistic
body "brothers". With the difference that in the family, life is
unified and communicated because there is a given relationship
of blood which functions as a natural bond of support, while
in the Church unity and communion of life are an achievement
of freedom.

The sharing of life's needs are an expression of real unity
and the realization of freedom, the concrete works of love
within the Church, over which those persons with a distinctive
spiritual gift preside, the *deacons*. In the first days of the
Church's life appeared the deacons of the eucharistic body
(Acts 6.1-7), whom the people chose and whom the Apostles
ordained in order to manage the work of ministry to the poor,
the sick, to all those members of the ecclesial community who
have a special need for care and provision. The deacons do not
celebrate the Eucharist, nor the mysteries, even in the name of
the Bishop. They minister at the celebration of the Eucharist,
but their chief rôle is to provide and care for those in need.
They have need of a separate ordination in order to carry out
this work, need of a distinct spiritual gift by the lifegiving

intervention of the Holy Spirit because in the Church caring activity is a manifestation of truth and the actualization of life, not altruism and utilitarian love for one another.

The spiritual gift which the deacons receive with their ordination is to serve the dynamic extension of the Eucharist in the whole life of the eucharistic body: to transform the service of practical needs for survival into "true life" of a loving communion in accordance with the triadic pattern of life. The provision and care for those in need within the Church is the organic fruit of the transformation of the individuals into persons who share life, into members of one body of life. "If one member suffers, every member suffers with it" (1 Cor 12.26). In the Church we care for those in need not in order to overcome and exterminate poverty, sickness, need, not in order to fight evil, not because we wish to "improve" or ease the conditions of life rationally or systematically, but just simply because we love. This is our radical difference from every state provision and moralistic "philanthropy". The difference is taken away if we deny the truth of the Church, if we consider it only as a "religion" and institution for the service of pious dispositions and emotional needs. Then we will use her caring work only in order to demonstrate the practical utility of the "institution", competing with the state social service organs and the utopian altruism of the moralists. Then, even the spiritual gift of ministry will remain unintelligible within the Church: the deacons will vocally adorn the celebration of the Eucharist, as a lower level in the bureaucratic hierarchy of the clergy, ushers in episcopal offices.

i. Synods, primacy and authority

The Church has its hierarchical arrangement and structure. It is an arrangement and structure which serves the realization and manifestation of the Church, that is the celebration of the Eucharist. But there is no administrative or organizational intentionality, at least, preceding the truth of the Church, its identity; for where such an intentionality does precede, it brings confusion and falsification of that truth and identity. The administrative arrangement and organizational structure and hierarchy of officers in the Church results from the celebration of the Eucharist and is concerned with this alone. Secondarily, they serve the dynamic extension of the Eucharist, the eucharistic transformation of the life of the faithful, the declaration and testimony of their faith to the world outside.

The initial presuppositions for the celebration of the Eucharist are the gathering of the baptized faithful and the presence of the president of the gathering, the Bishop or the presbyter acting for him. From the moment that there exist baptized faithful, the existence of a Bishop is the sole prerequisite for the formation of a Church. The Apostles established the first Bishops. The succession of the Bishops must have been the first very complicated problem of an organizational character which the Church confronted.

The Apostles transmitted to the first Bishops the spiritual gift for the eucharistic transformation of life, just as they received it themselves directly from Christ. The transmission of this spiritual gift occurs with the act of the "laying on of hands", the act of *ordination*, the invocation of the lifegiving activity of the Holy Spirit. When the generation of the Apostles had passed away, the only possible way to transmit this spiritual gift was to entrust this act to those who themselves possessed the gift, the existing Bishops. Without special theoretical elaboration, it was decided in practice that each new Bishop would be ordained by the Bishops of the immediately neighboring regions (the Bishops sharing a border with him), at least by three of them. The new Bishop was elected by the people of the vacant diocese, or by the neighboring Bishops, or even by the former Bishop of that same local Church. But the ordination was done exclusively by Bishops, three at least.

But the meeting of three Bishops for the ordination of a fourth constituted an event which formed a new body, an event of an assembly or *synod* of Bishops, as it came to be called. The synod was principally a liturgical event – it had in the first place a eucharistic character, not the character of a deliberation. The three or more Bishops who came together chiefly "concelebrated": But in the Eucharist there is one always who *offers* and *gives thanks* as president of the assembly. From these facts, then, the problem resulted of who among those who had come together in a synod of Bishops would have the presidency – who would preside over the common Eucharist.

On this subject, the practice of the Church followed, without theoretical sophisms, the mind and practice of the time and its historical environment: It was decided that the precedence in synod would be offered to the Bishop of the largest city, of the administrative and cultural centre of the region. They usually considered the administrative centre a "metropolis" (from the Greek words for "mother" and "city") of the region, and progressively the Bishop of this city took the additional title of "Metropolitan" taking on a few special obligations as well. Among the obligations of the Metropolitan, besides the presidency of the local synod, was some kind of arbitration in cases of disagreement or discord among the particular Bishops or between the priests and their Bishops.

The institution of the metropolitanates (the system of metropolitans) was developed more fully and methodically after the end of the persecutions and the recognition of the Christian Church as an official religion of the Roman Empire (*religio imperii*). Along side, there developed the institution of synods, within which the hierarchy of the Bishops took on a more definite shape as well. After the 5th century, the Bishops of the four large administrative and cultural centres of the Empire – Rome, Constantinople, Alexandria, and Antioch – took the title of Patriarch and a precedence of honour before all the other Metropolitans. To the four was added the Bishop of Jerusalem for reasons of respect and historical esteem. And so was formed the institution of the Pentarchy of Patriarchs which structured ecclesiastical life throughout the period of the single, undivided Christendom "throughout the world".

But the differentiation of titles of honorary precedence and of administrative responsibilities of the Metropolitans and Patriarchs never changed in the least detail the essential content of the rank of Bishop: Independently of the geographical extent or the political importance of his diocese and beyond every added title of Metropolitan or Patriarch, the Bishop remains, before anything else, president of and presiding at the Eucharist.

Therefore in any form of synod of Bishops, whether local (a synod of Bishops of one limited geographical region) or ecumenical (a synod of the whole of the Bishops of the Christian world), there is no distinction in voting or validity of opinion between Patriarchs, Metropolitans and simple Bishops. The Patriarch of Rome or of New Rome (Constantinople) has the same vote and his opinion the same strength as the vote and opinion of the Bishop of the smallest and least significant diocese.

This is so because in an ecclesiastical synod each Bishop who participates is not expressing and does not represent a population total or a geographic extension or political strength, just as he does not express his individual opinions and views more or less ingenious, more or less studied and consolidated. The Bishop conveys to the synod the witness and experiential certainty of the lay body in which he "presides over the Eucharist". He is the bearer of a lay experience, an experience of life. And the authenticity of this experience is the truth of the catholic (that is, of the whole) Church, it is the fulness and completion of the truth which the Church proclaims, independently of whether it is experienced by few or many, in a brilliant metropolis or in a humble town.

We have seen in the preceding pages that the synods formulate the boundaries or limits of the truth of the Church, that is the borders or the circumference of a truth which is not exhausted in its formulation, because it is not a theoretical "system" or "transcendental ideology", but is experienced and realized existentially in the dynamic of the life of the eucharistic body.

If, then, in a synod certain Bishops or even the whole of the Bishops express opinions, views and finally decisions unrelated to the experience of the eucharistic body, then the synod is annuled and the Bishops fall from their status – because finally the people are the judge and custodian of the ecclesial truth, the people are the bearer of the ecclesial experience of "true life".

Thus, within history, synods which aspired to have a general authority for the whole of Christendom – they were convoked as "ecumenical" and wanted to assert themselves as "ecumenical" – were rejected by the people, they were characterized as "robber" and "pseudo-synods". While others, much more temperate in their intentions, were recognized by the people as ecumenical, because the truth which they expressed and formulated was ecumenical and catholic.

This historical data, the denial of every institutionalized authority and the rejection of every infallible ruling principle within the Church, remains nevertheless unintelligible and inexplicable today, where our entire culture – our way of life – presupposes the subordination to the given authority of institutions and structures and ideologies and programmes and the exclusion of the people from the management of the essentials of life.

The womb of this despotic culture is the western European middle ages. There, progressively and with its culmination in the definitive separation of the West from the East (1054), the truth of the Church was separated from the event of the Eucharist and the experience of the lay body. The truth was separated from the experience of life to become a theoretical teaching, a given "dogma". The event of the Church was identified only with the hierarchy of the clergy, the administrative organization of the clergy to become a ruling structure and finally a state.

So, for the western European Christian, it seems inconceivable to subject an ecumenical synod of Bishops to the judgement of the lay body, since in its own history (and also mentality and temperament) the truth is given by authority, by a proceeding of objective enforcement, consequently by the existence of a given authority to which the people bow the head and submit – though sometimes they revolt and behead it.

A religious tradition of centuries shaped this mentality and temperament of the western European Christian; he had formed it to need, however, a certain objective authenticity for the definition of truth – a certain infallible *cathedra* or divinely inspired *Scripture* which would assure him psychologically of his individual possession of the truth. It led him to the

tragic dialectic of submission and rebellion, voluntary servitude
and revolution, which marks the entire modern European
history.

But for the tradition of undivided Christendom and its
historical continuity in Orthodoxy, it is not possible to
identify the truth of the Church with infallible institution
and authoritative structures without it being essentially falsi-
fied. Because authenticity and power furnish "objective"
assurance of individual certainty about the "truth", they
consequently fortify the ego, they isolate man in the fall, they
exclude him from the ecclesial mode of existence. And the
security of the ego is the more complete and rigid as the
coating of authority and of the "infallible" is more direct in
authoritatively imposing institutions and structures, with no
room for personal risk.

For the tradition of undivided Christendom and its historical
continuity in Orthodoxy, the truth of the Church is the event
of the Eucharist: the transformation of individual survival
into a life which is communicated as a gift of love and self-
transcendence – the loving renunciation of the ego if man is to
draw existence and identity from the fact that he is loved and
loves. You must "lose" in order to "save", says the Gospel,
lose your soul (Lk 9.24). The truth of the Church is the
destruction of every transitory self-defence and certainty in
order that life be saved; it is an achievement of life and
therefore a ceaseless risking, an adventure of freedom. If we
substitute a petrified institution in its authoritative self-
sufficiency for the dynamic of this achievement, then we will
have willingly exchanged life for death, truth for illusion or
deceit.

j. Religious alienation

God assumed the flesh of man in order to make it incorruptible
and to make it immortal – and this assumption is the existential
event which constitutes the Church, which shows it to be the
body of Christ. But flesh is not just the body of man, it is also
the entire complex of relations for his maintenance and
survival, the satisfaction of his manifold needs. The life and

truth of the Church are all of these relationships changed into Thanksgiving and loving communion. The Church assumes the whole human life, the biological and historical and cultural "flesh" of man, in order to transform it.

With its establishment as the "official religion" of the Roman Empire (*religio imperii*),[6] the Church also assumed the "flesh" of the religiosity of the world, sometimes transforming what she assumed and sometimes being subordinated to what she had assumed. Transformation and submission are phases in the adventure of human freedom, of *destruction* and *salvation*, of man's sin and of sanctification. To the extent that the truth of the Church is realized, with its centre of life the eucharistic transformation of the created, there appear theological and liturgical heights of patristic wisdom and holiness in history, the incomparable "semantics" of the Icons and the architecture of the churches, the monastic movement with its incompatibility with power structures. To the extent that people (clergy and lay) submit the truth of the Church to our natural need for "religion" – the metaphysical self-assurance of our individuality – the Church appears in history subject to the intentionality of the religious "institution", to the mind set of "authority" and of "efficiency", to the myopic pursuits of social ethics or of the politics of the moment.

With the establishment of the Church as the "official religion", the religious grades of "High Priest" and "priest" begin to appear in place of the titles of Bishop and Presbyter. A complicated administrative hierarchy is created and positions and titles are established unrelated to the eucharistic provenance of the ecclesial dignities and spiritual gifts, titles such as "archbishop", "exarch", "archimandrite", "chancellor", "protopriest", "archdeacon" – always with the object of differentiating access to some form of power. The clergy mimic the pompous salutations of the officers of the empire and with an increased dose of naïf exaggeration they establish greetings by degrees of holiness and reverence, such as "Most Holy", "Most reverend and learned", "Most venerable and

6By Theodosius the Great, on 27 February 380.

learned"[*], "Chief Steward", "Chief Deputy",[7] and a host of like pomposities.

Likewise the quarrels about the degrees of *primacy* of Bishops and dioceses begin, the disputes between the "distinguished thrones" of Rome and Constantinople, Constantinople and Alexandria, Alexandria and Antioch. The combination of ecumenical primacies with the idea of the empire would lead to the subjection of the Roman Church to the political ambitions of the Franks and later to the great Schism in Christendom. The same combination of ideas of empire with the episcopal primacies will appear in the national ambitions of the Slavic peoples ending in the haughty vision of Moscow, the Third Rome, and in the arbitrary multiplication in the institution of the Patriarchates. In the last two centuries, the idea of the *religio imperii* has taken historical flesh again in the form of an ethnic nationalism which submits the local Churches to the criteria and the intentionalities of tribalism and the policy of the régimes and governments of the time.[8]

All this and much more like it, has composed the "religious" part of the historical flesh of the Church, the current and transitory. They have no relationship with the truth of the Eucharist which forms the Church in a possibility of "eternal life" beyond time and place. But people who judge the Church by the standard of its historical mistakes and of the failure of institutions and structures or with the moral evaluation of its members and its leadership as the criteria are ignorant of this distinction. They try to evaluate the historical data to see if they can come to a conclusion about whether there are more positive or more negative aspects in the historical life of the Church.

People who judge "Christianity" for its moral return and its historical usefulness do not know what the Church and its truth are. They consider it a "religion" and an institution for

[7] *Literal* translations of honorific titles in use in the Orthodox Church: "Most Holy" – "Panayiotatos" is used, for instance, in addressing the Patriarch of Constantinople. Comparable titles occur in the West: "Your Holiness" for the Pope; "Your Grace" and "Most Reverend" for an archbishop. – tr.

[8] See C. Yannaras, *Truth and the Unity of the Church*, Athens, 1977 § 12: "The Institution of the Pentarchy Today" (in Greek).

the satisfaction of the "metaphysical needs of the people", and therefore they judge it by the measure of the "improvement" of the morals and conventions of our mortal life. They do not suspect that beyond temporary "improvements" or failures, in every eucharistic gathering mortal human life is changed into a life of immortality and incorruptibility. The unworthiness of individuals, the sins of laity and clergy, the scandals of leading persons in the Church do not suspend this transformation – it is enough that there exist even the least leaven in the lay body which shares consciously in the Eucharist.

The Gospel forewarns that the Church or the Kingdom of God is a "net" with "rotten and good" (Mt 13.47), a "field" with wheat and tares (Mt 13.25). We are saints and sinners, equally members of the Church – just, pious, ascetics together with robbers, prostitutes and the dissolute. We are all found within the Church, not in order to improve our virtues or to "correct our characters", but because we thirst for life free from corruption and death. We know that whether we are virtuous or sinners, we are equally mortal – the common sin of all of us is death, the fact that our natural individuality and hypostasis will disappear one day in the ground (since "sin" does not mean a transgression of laws or commandments, but "missing the mark" and "privation", a failure as to the goal or "end" of our existence). We share in the Church because we thirst for life, the loving fullness of life. The virtue of mortal man does not interest us, but the eternity of the repentant man.

Within the Church, our strength is "perfected in weakness" (2 Cor 12.9) – the great strength of the Church is our historical failures and sins. Why are sins "strength"? Above all, because the recognition of our own failure and weakness, just like respect for the failure and weakness of the other, is the foundational condition of freedom, it is a denial of the totalitarianism which derives every "perfection" from rational prescriptions. Let anyone at all dare to "sin" within a political party, in an organized ideology, in some business activity: He will pay without forgiveness (sometimes with his blood) for the transgression of the "letter" or of the "orders of the centre" or of the interests of the business. Today especially, within a world and culture which everywhere runs after success, accuracy and "perfection", the Church is the only place which preserves the last chance for man's freedom, the freedom of his failure and his weakness.

But the strength of the Church is made perfect in weakness chiefly because only with the recognition of human inadequacy can we transpose the possibility of life into the love of God which "raises the dead". Isolation in self-sufficiency, satisfaction in our virtue, our efficiency, results, sound judgement, do not leave room for the leap of self-denial and self-transcendence which free the lifegiving possibility of love. As much as we expect fruits of life (salvation, justification, immortality) from our religiosity, our ethics, our institutional productivity, by so much we distance ourselves from the possibility of "true life". On the contrary, the individual sins of each one of us, together with every phase and mark of bankruptcy in the human representation of the Church – immoral Bishops, robber Synods, political trafficking in the ecclesial truth – richly disappoint us, just as they confirm the utopian character of our moralistic ambitions for the "renewal" of mankind.

The eternal life which the Church announces begins from the sign where the existential possibilities of the created end – every tendency to self-existence and every individual claim of life. Salvation from death is a work for the uncreated, not a work for the created; it is Grace, a spiritual gift, and not an achievement of nature. It is given on that level of existence, when nature is free from need, the need for self-existence, self-maintenance. Then the possibility of the triadic mode of existence is opened to man: life as a self-transcendence of love.

This is the testimony of the Church which found its historical incarnation especially in the persons of the *martyrs* and the *ascetics*. The real evidence of the martyrs and its historical extension, the struggle of the ascetics, marks the ecclesial life definitively, precisely because they preserve the truth of the Church unsullied by falsifications: Life is not individual survival, but the final self-denial to the point of death, by a "transport of love" for the Person of God in Christ Jesus.

10

Orthodoxy

a. Apophaticism and ritualism

In the language of contemporary man, the word "orthodoxy" has the sense of adherence to some dogma, to the letter of an ideology. It is almost synonymous with "conservatism", persistence in a given form. Someone is orthodox who remains faithful to the genuine and authentic formulation of a teaching, in opposition to those who deviate and falsify its original interpretation.

And so, every dogmatic ideology – religious, social, or political – also has its orthodoxy. We speak, for instance, of Lutheran, Freudian, or Marxist orthodoxy, if we mean the persistence (conservative and usually sterile) in the formulations of Luther himself, or of Freud, or of Marx – the contrast of this persistence with later versions and creative reshapings of the initial ideas.

Usually the invocation of orthodoxy happens with a boasting about faithfulness to what is genuine and authentic. Boasting means a demand for common recognition of and reverence for what has been handed on, but also for those people who maintain and represent it. Thus, orthodoxy comes to function as a means for justifying not so much conservative ideas as conservative people – to serve often for the psychological veiling of cowardice or spiritual sterility. Those who will not risk or cannot create something new in life fasten themselves fanatically to some orthodoxy. They draw authority, authenticity and, finally, power as representatives and administrators of genuineness – protectors of the forms, interpreters of the letter. They transform, finally, any orthodoxy whatever into a "procrustean bed" where they mutilate life in order to make it fit the demands of their dogma.

This interpretation of orthodoxy and the symptoms which accompany it are a consequence of a particular understanding of truth and of the possibilities of approaching truth. It presupposes man's ability individually to possess the truth and consequently to transform it into an object which he can dominate.

For truth to be transformed into an object of possession, it must have a given and definite character, it must be identified with its formulation, with the "letter" of the formulation – the truth must find in its formulation its immutable boundaries. The identification with the definite formulation objectifies the truth: it makes it an object which the understanding can possess and rule. And insistence on orthodoxy, on the first and authentic objectification, is the fullest form of possession of the truth.

Such an understanding of truth and of the possibilities of approaching truth characterize and also provide the foundation for our civilization today – the so called western European culture in its now world-wide dimensions. It is, nevertheless, completely unrelated to the Church and to ecclesial orthodoxy.

The "apophaticism" of the ecclesial truth, of which we have spoken in previous pages, excludes any objectified understanding of orthodoxy whatsoever. The truth is not exhausted in its formulation, the formulation is simply a boundary or border of truth, a "garment" or a "guard" of truth. Truth is the reality which does not contradict itself – the final truth is the life which is not refuted by death. Therefore knowledge of the truth is not attained by comprehension of the formulations, but with the sharing in the event of truth, in the truth of life, in the immediacy of experience.

b. Heresy and catholicity

In the history of the Church, the term "orthodoxy" made its appearance to distinguish the truth from "heresy". But heresy as much as orthodoxy applies to facts, not theoretical principles. Heresy is the fact of separation from the ecclesial body, the formation of a group unrelated to the local eucharistic gathering, the real denial of the ecclesial mode of existence, which is the unity and communion of love. On the other hand, orthodoxy is the truth of the *catholic* Church, as it is realized and revealed in every local eucharistic gathering. Every local Church is the catholic Church (an event and experience of catholicity), where it sums up and incarnates the whole truth of the Church, all of the truth, that is life in its fullness "in Christ" – all the spiritual gifts of life which the Holy Spirit grants.

The evidence from the texts of the first centuries which confirm that the *catholic* Church is the criterion of orthodoxy, and not orthodoxy the criterion of the catholic Church is very explicit. [1] The presupposition of orthodoxy is sharing in the catholic Church, not insistence on the correctness of theoretical formulations. The event and the experience of catholicity preceed the theoretical formulations – the theoretical formulations are provoked by heresies; these require the Church to express in definite formulations the experience of her truth. The rightness of the truth and of the faith preceed both chronologically and essentially. It is assured by sharing in the experience of the catholic Church and simply the covering or the boundaries of its defence are in its intellectual formulation.

c. The criterion of orthodoxy

However, heresy is shown not only as an event (in the act of *schism*), but also as a theoretical teaching. The heretics teach a "truth" which does not correspond to the experience and faith of the catholic Church. This non-correspondence with the experience and faith of the catholic Church is the criterion for the differentiation of heresy from orthodoxy, a criterion which becomes an attempt to seek objectification in the definitions of the Councils and in the writings of the church

[1]See J. Zizioulas, *The Unity of the Church*, pp. 126 ff.

Fathers, while never ceasing to presuppose the dynamic indeterminacy of life, the immediacy of experience.

The definite formulations of truth and the dynamic indeterminacy of the experience of the truth are two elements, however, which are inconsistent at the level of logical thought. They can, though, be harmonized at the level of life and of the hypostatic bearer of life which is the person: Therefore the criterion of ecclesial orthodoxy is the experience and faith of the catholic Church incarnate in the persons of the saints. And the saints of the Church are not distinguished on the basis of their moral superiority, but on the basis of the revelation and portrayal of the truth in their persons. The criterion of truth is ecclesial catholicity, and the measure of catholicity the integration of the spiritual gifts of life in the persons of the saints.

The adaptation of these measures and criteria for the separation of orthodoxy from heresy is an unbearable scandal for the rational mind: It leaves uninterpreted a large number of details in church history or at least complicates what we consider a logical interpretation of these details. Often, for instance, heretics are in the majority, but finally it is recognized that the Church with the numerical minority is *catholic*. We speak of recognition of orthodoxy by the body of the people, but still the criterion of recognition is not objective and defined, it is not the opinion of the majority. Sometimes heresy imposes itself not only numerically, but also chronologically; it appears for a long interval of time as the authentic truth and faith of the Church. But orthodoxy returns in the end triumphant, even if it has been preserved in the person of only one man. Emperors have fought orthodoxy and let loose persecutions against the orthodox; a very few synods of Bishops have defined dogmas in an anti-orthodox and heretical way. But the opposite as well: secular rulers or even clergy imposed dogmatic orthodoxy with force, the orthodoxy of the letter, while the same were tragically lacking the ethos of orthodox truth. And from all this "external" and "internal" undermining, orthodoxy finally is preserved – or at least has been preserved for centuries as a living lay consciousness of faithfulness to the experience and witness of the Apostles and saints.

How, then, is the preservation of this indeterminate criterion which divides orthodoxy from heresy accomplished? How are all the above symptoms and a great many others related to them to be interpreted, while no standard of objective and authentic affirmation of the truth is present? The answer is found in the insistence of the Church on identifying truth with life and life with its only hypostatic bearer which is the person – in the refusal of the Church to substitute intellectual schemata, moral codes, authoritative structures of authenticity for the immediacy of experience and relationship. In this way, orthodoxy is won or lost, just as every gift of life is won or lost: an authentic love, an achievement of artistic expression, a dynamic beginning of knowledge.

This preservation or destruction remains inaccessible to the "objective" criteria of science and historiography – just as on the other hand the living function of language remains inaccessible to these same criteria with its historical transformations, or the creative manifestations of art and their social "semantics".

d. The Greek contribution

Nevertheless, we must not forget that the Church developed historically within a world and culture that was Greek or hellenized, which had an understanding of truth very different from that of the demand for "objectivity". From Heraclitus to the neo-platonists, knowledge was verified as an event of communion: "everything that we share, we know to be true; what we have that is peculiar to us, we know to be false".[2] Knowledge is proved true, only when it is verified by common experience – only when by its announcement we share with others, understand and are understood, are in tune with the common experiential certitude.

It is not, then, the individual understanding which constitutes the approach to truth, but only its social verification, the event of participation in the general reason. Without this theory of knowledge which looks to the dynamics of the

---

[2] Heraclitus, Frag. Diels-Kranz I, p. 148, 29-30.

society, we cannot approach either Greek philosophy or Greek art or the communal achievement of the ancient city state, the ideal of democracy of the Greeks.

Ecclesial orthodoxy shaped and developed its apophatic character within a world and culture which was adapted in almost every feature to the criteria of apophatic knowledge. The greatest heresies of the first eight centuries – great in the number of partisans and in temporal duration – never touched this fundamental assumption of the historical manifestation of orthodoxy, which is the apophaticism of ecclesial theology. Therefore these heresies did not survive historically (some few groups of Monophysites which are preserved to our day do not represent more than a fanatical adherence to a certain defective terminology and language), because they did not touch and did not falsify the mode of life, the dynamic and social interpretation of the truth which founded and organized the life of the Greek or hellenized world.

e. The Western deviation

The first heretical differentiation which not merely survives historically, but has transformed radically the course of human history is one which denies the fundamental presupposition of orthodoxy, the apophaticism of truth. It was born in the area of western Europe, and established its novelties and opinions on a new understanding of knowledge and the verification of knowledge. It led to the only schism which has proved historically incurable, and it shaped finally another mode of life, that is, another civilization definitely incompatible with the dynamic of orthodox ecclesial truth.

Nevertheless, the denial of the apophaticism of knowledge existed as a foundation or seed in the legal mentality of the Roman tradition. Rome is the cradle of the science of Law, of its systematic development and cultivation. And the persistence in juridical scrutinies inescapably accustomed it to an objectification of cases, to the substitution of the dynamic indeterminacy of life with schemata and definitive models of life. The uniqueness of the event is understood by its classification in the objectivity of the general case – the verification of experience is assured by refuge in its schematic definition.

Augustine is surely the first great stage in the theoretical foundation of the rejection of apophaticism. He did not have a Greek education – he did not even know the Greek language. He was a student chiefly of Cicero's legal thought, of Tertullian and of Ambrose of Milan. He transferred the mentality of the claims of objectivity in justice to the area of the claims for certain knowledge: just as the laws of justice fix the boundaries of the objective and effective assurance of social harmony, so also the definite, inescapably schematic – but commonly received – defining of truth assures the effective objectivity of knowledge and constitutes a kind of law of truth.

And so, for the first time in history, truth is identified with its formulation and knowledge or the possession of truth with the individual understanding of this formulation. The truth is separated from the dynamic of life, it is identified with the concept, with right reasoning. Already in the writings of Augustine the fundamental consequences of this radical change in the understanding of the truth are present – consequences which will constitute the later base of the social and cultural life of the West: right reasoning replaces the dynamic indeterminacy of life; life enters the forecourt of "logic" (*ratio*), logic is raised to a final authority, either in the form of moral rules or as a command of social and political practice. Moralism and political totalitarianism, these two formal products of western European civilization, have their explicit roots in the thought of Augustine.

Still, Augustine would remain rather a solitary heretical thinker, with his novelties overlaid by the wonderful example of his conversion and moral about-face, if in the 9th century the Franks had not discovered the meaning of his heretical teaching: the ambition of Charlemagne to found a second Roman empire in the West, totally independent of the hellenized East, led above all to the search for a differentiated cultural base – since at the time the cultural base was also the presupposition of political unity. And the evidence of the historians is unanimous, that Augustine was used as such a base – exclusively Latin, without Greek influences.

From Augustine, the Franks drew the elements of a religious differentiation which led to the great schism of West and East in 1054. It is not simply the letter of the heretical deviations or only the legal mentality and the accompanying rationalism which they offered for this differentiation. There exists, from all that, something much more drastic in the augustinian teaching: the preponderance of the religious element over the ecclesial element. Sharing in the truth of the Church presupposes the renunciation of individuality, of the ego, the transformation of life into a loving communion, in accordance with the triadic original of true life. To the contrary, religiosity is always individual: it "improves", comforts, satisfies, and assures the individual. Augustine conceived of and preached the Church as a religion, something which convinces the human understanding rationally, which aids in the individual self-possession and morality, and which offers the individual the protection and assurance of a higher authority.

The schism of 1054 opened the road for the most radical, perhaps, historical falsification of Christianity, which is its being turned into a "religion". Therefore, the completion of the differentiations which the Franks introduced would bring to light not simply a new empire or a new and transitory heresy, but another civilization introduced for the first time in history.

The next phase of this differentiation is *scholasticism*, an astonishingly vigorous phase of development of the augustinian inheritance. Within just two centuries, the 12th and 13th, the scholastics completed the radical reversal of the criteria and presuppositions of the ecclesial theology, seeing that they rejected the Greek origin and seal of these presuppositions: They refused the apophaticism of theological formulation, the priority of life and of the hypostatic bearer of life which is the person in his existential otherness and freedom. They returned to the ancient Greek ontology (to the priority which the conceptual understanding had of essence, to the essentialist, logical definition of existence, its "absolute destiny"). But while they returned to the ancient Greek ontology, which the Greek Fathers had rejected,[3] the scholastics rejected the ancient Greek gnosiology, which the Greek Fathers had adopted. They were familiar with the augustinian understanding of knowledge, the exhaustion of knowledge in the capacities of the individual understanding. They defined the truth as a "coincidence of the thought with the object to be understood" – knowledge is verified with this co-incidence alone, the truth is transformed into an intellectual achievement.

Selections and rejections made by the scholastics, novelties and theortical schematizations all serve to complete the change on the level of experience and assimilation: the passage from the ecclesial to the religious level. The art of the period mirrors very clearly the change to be completed by theoretical formulations, making the Church in the West into a "religion". When at the beginning of the 12th century the gothic style appears in the architecture of churches, it is obvious that it has come to express (in a manner however talented) a change, which has already been completed in what is done inside the church. When from the 13th century ecclesial iconography is abandoned definitively to the joy of religious art (the delight of the individual senses and the incitement of individual emotions), it is again obvious that the fact reflects a change in the way life and the world are viewed.

f. The historical change

Scholastic rationalism, in the centuries of its height, is not just a philosophical or theological current and system. It is a "closed" dogmatic ideology, with the Roman Catholic Church as its officially established bearer: It interprets definitively and conclusively the whole natural and historical reality and plans this interpretation with "axioms", "principles" and "laws" of rationalistic certainty. Rational objectivity

[3]For the preceding, see pp. 42 ff. A more extensive treatment is found in C. Yannaras, *Outline for an Introduction to Philosophy*, 2nd ed. (Athens, Domos, 1988), in Greek. Also in French as *Philosophie sans rupture* (Editions "Labor et Fides", Genève, 1986).

lends authority to the institutional bearer of the ideology, and the authority of the institutional bearer validates the rational plan.

This double correlation finds its political expression in the theocratic vision of the universal rule of the papacy, in the concentration of every spiritual, legislative, judical and political power (*plenitudo potestatis*) in the hands of the Roman pontiff. Thomas Aquinas gave a metaphysical character to this pure power: in the *Summa Theologiae* (1266-1272) he introduced the principle of papal infallibility, thus establishing the dignity of infallible leadership, the absolute prerogative of administering truth which is not succeptible to debate. A few years earlier in 1233, Pope Gregory IX had established the institution of the Holy Inquisition (*Inquisitio*), putting the prerogative of infallibility into practice. And in 1252, Innocent IV in a papal bull had sanctioned torture as a method of investigation in the trials of heretics, completing the example for all later totalitarianisms to annihilate those with a differing opinion.

But three centuries later, while the dearly paid for *Reformation* radically disputed almost in their entirety all the details of the historical falsification of the Christian message of salvation, it did not manage to touch the core or creative cause of these falsifications: it did not touch the ontology and epistemology of Roman Catholicism but remained blindly subjected to Augustine, replacing institutional authority with the "infallibility" of the texts.

From Augustine to Thomas Aquinas and up to Calvin the new version of ecclesiastical orthodoxy had been completed: orthodoxy means now conformity with institutionalized, sovereign ideology – which is sovereign because it is logically and socially and metaphysically obligatory. It still means faithfulness to the letter of the ideological formulation, while it guarantees the individual possession of the truth. It means finally the subjection to the power structures in which it is expressed and the authority of the orthodoxy safeguarded.

The fact that the West did not lay claim to the characterization of orthodoxy for its reckoning, might, though, be thought typical. It preferred the characterization of *catholicity*,

giving an exclusively quantitative and geographic and cen-
tralized and organizational content to the term. The word
"orthodoxy" was preserved in order to characterize the
churches of the east who remained faithful to the apostolic
and patristic Tradition, theology and practice of ecclesial life.

But the fidelity of the Greek or hellenized world of the
Christian East to the original ecclesial orthodoxy ceased very
early to be incarnate in a concrete historical frame of political
and cultural autonomy. From the beginning of the 13th
century, hordes of Frankish crusaders subverted and subjected
the orthodox Greek East to Latin rule (1204). The forces of
Hellenism offered one last resistance, they succeeded in
recovering their historical axis or centre, Constantinople, but
they were now irreparably exhausted.

There followed the Turkish conquest (1453) and for four
hundred years the Greek world sank into a painful historical
speechlessness, under the foot of the most brutal barbarity. It
is a matter of the political (and in large measure, cultural)
disappearance of the Greeks from the historical stage. Ecclesiastical orthodoxy was preserved, in spite of religious persecutions which the Turks let loose from time to time and the
efforts of forced conversion of the Christian populations to
Islam which brought pages of early Christian martyrdom back
to life. Orthodoxy was identified organically with the popular
cultural consciousness and identity; it became a popular ethos;
it differentiated the Greek virtually both from the Turk of
another religion as much as from the heterodox Frank.

In these four martyr centuries, the only historical relationship of the European West with the Greek East was the
successive waves of missionaries who strove tirelessly to
proselytize the orthodox to Roman Catholic or Protestant
dogmas. The developments in world history which, in the
interval, were completed in the West and literally changed the
course of human history were not followed by the enslaved
Greeks, except only as an echo of wonderful achievements – it
was not possible for the achievements to be evaluated and
judged by the criteria of life and truth of the orthodox ecclesial
Tradition.

Without exaggeration, one could speak of a cosmogony which was accomplished in the West in the four hundred years of the historical silence of Hellenism. Let us recall, briefly, the development of the physical sciences and of technology, the discoveries of new lands and the influx of wealth into Europe, the radical philosophical ideas and the consequent political and social liberalism, the extension of the middle class and the revolutions for the vindication of its rights, the new understanding of the state and power, the appearance of capitalism and the astonishing spread of the use of machines in manufacturing.

A chief characteristic of these historical changes is the attempt of European man to rule over the natural and historical reality of his own powers and capacities, without recourse to metaphysical dependence and religious justifications of his endeavours. The progressive unchaining from the authority of the Roman Church and, finally, the antithetical distinction of religious and secular elements of life became the basic marks of the period of "modern times" in Europe. The augustinian tradition and scholasticism had taught the autonomy of the intellectual capacity of the individual, and European man claimed in consequence this autonomy by rejecting even the metaphysical reference or bond. With the clearest and universally acknowledged religious bases, western European culture appeared, after the so called "renaissance" of the 14th and 15th centuries, if not radically antireligious, then in any case with, as its characteristic mark, the polar oppositions of transcendent and worldly, faith and knowledge, sacred and "profane", authority and research, revelation and experience, submission and debate.

g. The Westernization of the East

The echo of the historical developments in the western European area reached the enslaved Hellenism by means of one channel especially: the scholars of the time who had studied in the universities of Europe. They maintained contact with the European centres and followed the spiritual currents and the social transmutations. All these, without exception, nourished an unlimited admiration for what was being accomplished in the West. In contrast with the "darkness" of slavery, the poverty and illiteracy which ruled in the East, Europe was "enlightened": there were "the lights" of culture, progress, superiority. There was no critical distancing, caution or discussion in the scholarly Greeks of that time, just an immense affirmation and enthusiasm for whatever was western.

Only when purely atheistic ideas began to appear in the West did there begin certain reservations or even reactions chiefly in ecclesiastical circles about the "new ideas", just as about the sciences (anyhow to the positive sciences) which lead to these ideas. But such reactions had no relationship to the differences of Hellenism and West or ecclesial orthodoxy and heresy. They are typical symptoms of an ideological and social conservatism, copied exactly from the conservatism of the clergy and of the religious individuals of the West. The reaction does not proceed from a critical comparison of different criteria or standards for the evaluation of cultural achievements.

The stance of the Greek scholars before the West is not limited to the uncritical enthusiasm and unlimited admiration for the "lights" of Europe. It proceeds to an equally uncritical assumption of ideas, and also of the criteria and the mentality of westerners. It is a question of a whole phenomenon of westernization of the Greek mind, without the least suspicion of the possible dynamics of the Greek cultural tradition, the important differences which separated the Greek from the western ontology and theory of knowledge, and the socio-political consequences of these differences.

The westernization of the spiritual leadership of the enslaved Hellenism seals the historical evolution of the 19th century: the conventional Greek mini-state which arose from the liberating revolution of 1821 was organized as a faithful copy of the institutions and structures of western European life and was founded in dependence on and under direct control of the European powers. Together with the other institutions – political, administrative, educational – the structures of ecclesiastical life were essentially westernized, such as the assumptions for the cultivation of theology. And so, the phenomenon was repeated which had happened previously in orthodox Russia with the reformation of Peter the Great in the 18th century: an orthodox people suffered the imposition from above of the western way of organizing and administering theology and popular piety.

h. Orthodoxy and the west today

This brief and perhaps exaggeratedly sketchy historical retrospection intends only to note the problems which are combined with the elucidation, presence and witness of ecclesial orthodoxy in our days. The distinction of Orthodoxy and West has ceased to be discernible – it is not self-evident. The West no longer has geographical limits, it is everywhere. It is the first civilization in history with real universal dimensions. And civilization means the specific theoretical assumptions, ideological or dogmatic, which are translated consciously or unconsciously into an attitude of life, into an everyday way of life.

Today, even in the so called orthodox countries, the culture is western; the everyday way of life has the roots of its historical formation in the western metaphysic, reaching back to Aquinas and Augustine. Thus orthodoxy seems to be limited just to individual convictions, leaving unaffected the activity of life, the historical incarnation of the truth. Orthodoxy is changed into an abstract teaching, a fleshless dogma, a maintenance of forms of worship and external forms.

But, if these are the "objective" data for the definition of the problem, the reality of life is not exhausted, however, in the phenomenology of symptoms. Certainly, the dynamic of ecclesial truth can remain in suspension and orthodoxy voiceless for many decades or even centuries. But the absence of a concrete historical dynamic – the absence of timely evidence of orthodoxy, incarnate in a concrete cultural realization – does not mean that either the seed of the ecclesial truth or the sap which furthers its growth is dead. Somewhere life is secretly giving birth and sometime the buried seed will shake the firm ground.

In the meantime, for the present generation of orthodox at least, there is only one central subject of study and life: the re-estimation of Orthodoxy and the West, the analysis and investigation of the manifold implications of this re-estimation and, especially, its humble and crucified experiencing, the search for a solution incarnate in the hypostatic manifestations of life, in the persons of the saints. Let us not forget that a criterion of orthodoxy is ecclesial catholicity and the standard of catholicity the totality of the spiritual gifts of life in the persons of the saints.

The re-evaluation of Orthodoxy and the West is not a matter of abstract theoretical rivalries, nor of historical contrasts of institutions, and therefore it cannot be overcome with frater-nal efforts at reconciliation of separated Christian churches. The theological differences are not interesting in themselves, but their direct consequences in life and in historical activity. The orthodox consciousness has to answer at least the chal-lenge of western atheism and nihilism, which literally sweep – and not by chance – the Christendom of the West which has been made into a "religion". The critique of religion by the Enlightenment and liberalism, Marxism, Freudianism, atheistic existentialism, scientific agnosticism, seems inescapably precise and historically justified. The question is, what answers of life and what dynamic of life does orthodoxy have to bring against this critique.

The re-evaluation seems frighteningly disproportionate, as the hardened structures of a culture with very powerful authoritative imposition on the organization of human life are opposed on the one side, and on the other the orthodox consciousness which is barely preserved in the liturgical experience and the theological word. It is, in fact, a question of the "grain of wheat" which dissolves, lost within the earth – this is the Orthodoxy of our days. Only, this death is the hope and faith of the Orthodox. The problem of orthodox witness today is a problem of distinguishing between the lifebearing grave of the "grain of wheat" and the hopeless corruption with no way out which corrodes openly the structures of the civilization of heresy.

Today, the dead end of western culture is no longer theoretical: it is contained as anxiety and absurdity in the everyday way of life. This civilization of the "balance of terror" has managed to threaten life in general, of rationalistic programs for the "general happiness", of the drugs of the outcasts, of the debility of consumption, of the enthralment of human existence by totalitarian ideologies.

Within this death, the Church remains in expectation of the resurrection of the dead. As the orthodox liturgical tradition is preserved and "functions", even if hidden in unknown parishes or dioceses, and the theological witness is uttered with the way of life which worship perserves as its pivot, a civilization at the antipodes of that of the West survives secretly and one word, ecumenical and salvific for man, is being brought dynamically to birth.

Index